To do List Formula:

How to win laziness, overcome procrastination, increase your productivity and improve time management on a daily basis

Table of Contents

Introduction

Suppose someone calls you for an advice about being overwhelmed. That person might say, "I always have much to do, but I never know where to start, and then I do nothing." What would your response be during this conversation? Would it sound like:" you know what? I used to feel that way too, but I haven't in a couple of years and I am going to share with you what's changed, and what's now happening in my life that I don't experience that problem anymore."

Or you might as well be the victim who needs a bailout for this problem. Well, the good news is I am going to be sharing with you proven methods of selecting a task ahead of time by making an effective to do list.

The biggest thing to remember is why you make to-do lists in the first place, and that is to get the tasks out of your head as well as the associated worries that come with them, and free up that valuable mind of yours to do more important things.

The following is a combination of techniques that I have smashed together to help create a to-do list that really works:

Use Paper for Short-Term Goals

Digital tools, in my opinion, are for planning over long stretches of time, or for planning larger projects. But digital lists have one major disadvantage that makes them really bad for day to day planning; they are never-ending. Give you no idea of how far along you are, whereas a paper list can also be a progress bar for your day.

You should allow yourself no more than a piece of paper with few lines to lay up your to-do list. This will force you to prioritize. Unimportant stuff is not going to find its way on to the list because you simply don't have all the time in the world.

In addition, paper allows the crossing off of items in a much more satisfying way than a digital list, so you could happily move to the next item.

Do some cherry picking

This may probably sound like some kind of lousy advice but trust me, it is magic.

You put something important on your list that you want to do. Maybe it is kind of quick and easy. You should do that item first because the sooner you can cross something off, especially the more important things, the better. You get a rush of dopamine every time you accomplish something, and that is a neurohormone that can in turn, make you more productive. This technique is called priming.

You don't need to finish the list.

Now at first, it seems to fly right in the face of something I mentioned earlier, which is that your list is your progress bar for your day. So how would you not feel like a total failure when you only get two things done on your list in a day? You do what I do. You look at that incomplete list and you don't let it discourage you.

Ultimately you can only do as much as you can do in one day, no matter how long your list is.

Efficiently and effectively making your next list

Whenever you need to start a new list, move the items that are important and leave the ones that are not. This is a good time to decide what items are falling into the realm of unimportant, and simply don't do them. Now we have a nice shiny new list with only important items in them.

Let us go on to what may be the most important tip of all.

Draw little boxes with shadows.

As you are making a list, draw a little box next to each major item, a little empty checkbox. And then, when you are finishing up the list, go back to each box and then draw a little drop shadow.

Drawing a little drop shadow is a peaceful sort of mini-meditation exercise. It is pretty focusing and calming, and it has three little bonuses:

First, there is the application of the dopamine rush that comes with crossing items off, because now you have to check little boxes too.

Secondly, when you enter into this meditative state, it will give your mind time to focus, and subconsciously deal with the items on that list.

Thirdly, like clockwork, when you are in these state, new and important items will come into your head.

Chapter 1: Characteristics of To-Do Lists.

Most of us have our own styles of to-do lists, but organizational experts have discovered that some ways of putting an effective list together are better than others.

Nonetheless, there are common characteristics of all good to-do lists that contribute to our productivity and reduce our stress.

Here are ten characteristics of the best to-do lists, gleaned from research about hundreds of lists over the years, and the latest literature and science on the subject.

Serious preparation work

The most effective to-do lists start with you taking a brief time out to write down all the tasks that you need to complete. If you want to emulate this, pick a specific time period for your planning. Many business people like to plan per quarter of the year; others live their lives according to seasons. Still others prefer just to look a month ahead, and others a week. Estimates are that to do this part of the list-making like the pros, it will take you between one and two hours.

Task breakdown

Once the tasks are all laid before you, study them to see what's involved. Are they one-act tasks, or complicated, multifaceted tasks? If they fall into the latter class, then they need to be broken down into as many small steps as possible.

Specific details

For example, the agenda of the very effective list writer does not say "Meet with Jack at 9 a.m. It says "meet with Jack, bring coffee, cream, no sugar, and persuade him to sign off on his website content. Negotiate at least three weeks more in timing before a prototype of the site needs to be shown."

Prioritization

We tend to think of prioritization as numbering 1, 2 and 3 and so on, and while that is essential for daily lists, for a longer-term list it is sometimes more useful to simply designate whether the task is urgent or essential but not urgent, or needed but neither urgent nor essential. Just using your own code or the initials U, I, and NU would work.

Adaptability to your life

This is a very controversial area when it comes to list making. Science supports that short daily lists with no more than three to four items are most effective for the majority of people. But when it comes to your own life, don't be governed by other people's rules. Figure out what works best for you. Many managers who must stay on top of a multitude of projects find that having a longer list that ensures some progress is made daily. is more stress-reducing than having to select just three projects a day to work on.

Advance planning

A common characteristic of effective to-do listers is their insistence of never ending one day without planning the next. You may decide that marking off your priorities for the next day is something that closes your day well for you in your workplace, or you may find your ability to make decisions and focus more keenly comes after you've reached the quiet point of your evening. Whatever system works best for you is fine. Either way, you will find your morning gets started more effectively if you ensure that your priority list is completed and waiting for you when you awaken.

Choice of paper or technology

This again is a matter of personal choice. Many people who use the traditional list writing skill of pen to paper feel a sense of calmness and control infused in them as they go through their daily listing exercise. Others find it much more efficient to use even a simple Microsoft Word document list or one of the many other electronic options from "Evernote" to "Toodledo" to "Remember the Milk".

Unique solutions

A president or prime minister, for example, has a far larger list of projects to keep moving along than the average person. They may need more complex technical programs that do some of their scheduling and send them alerts frequently. If your life has become unbearably complicated, consider seeking organizational solutions that are customized for your situation.

Transitioning across life's borders

Our average days are usually a blend of what we do for ourselves and for others. We move seamlessly through the art of handling our own personal grooming, making breakfast for ourselves and others, picking up a colleague and heading to work, completing our work tasks, remembering to call midway through the day to check on a sick friend, meeting a colleague for lunch, and rushing home a half-hour early to be there for the air conditioning service technician.

What distinguishes the to-do list of really effective people is their acknowledgment that our lives must move effortlessly through various segments to blend into a whole. Instead of handling only work tasks, they also jot down their other key appointments, understanding that for life to operate smoothly, we must be able to integrate all of its parts.

Personalized techniques

List-making, as those who do it can effectively confirm, is primarily the art of remembering what needs to be done, deciding what is most important, and then completing the tasks at hand. Many people report that the most challenging aspects of the three pillars of list-making is making the decision about what is most important.

Some people develop unique techniques to help them decide what should be number one on their list. They ask themselves: Which item on my list, if not completed today, is going to cause me the most grief later on? Others ask which task has the most revenue associated with it, or the most warmth of personal accomplishment. Create your own assessment system based on your own values and you will find the decision becomes much easier.

Chapter 2: The Power of The List

With plenty of options out there in the world, from fancy iPhone apps to calendar systems and beyond, I have never found something as flexible, powerful, and effective as a simple written to-do list.

There are four main reasons to create a to-do list:

First, it serves as a reinforcement of my highest and best use of my time.

Sure, it's a list of the stuff I need to get done... But it goes beyond that. By writing down my daily priorities in a certain manner, I am constantly filtering each opportunity presented to me throughout my day through a very powerful lens: the lens of my dreams. In my experience from working with dozens upon dozens of clients one-on-one, and in groups and workshops, we spend very little time thinking about our dreams.

Yes, we think about the future: how we're going to pay for college, what we need to pick up at the grocery store for meals in the coming week, or whether it's time to replace our oil filter. But we don't think about our brightest future. We are so concerned about the now and what's going to happen tomorrow and next week, that the big stuff gets put on hold. Of course, the problem with that is that we never seem to get to it. A to-do list, when prepared and used in the way I'll teach you, will bring those bright secret golden dreams out of the shoebox in the closet and into the light, and even into today. You're going to be totally jazzed when you see how easy it is to start building that future you've always dreamed about.

Second, people get distracted. There are millions upon millions of calls for our attention each and every day. Having a concrete reminder of your focus for the next 24 hours pulls you back home again and again. There's no excuse for not writing the next chapter in your book because you "forgot." It was right there in front of you, hopefully something you looked at several times over the course of the day.

Third, a to-do list is a black-and-white (sometimes literally) assessment of whether or not you are getting the right things done. When your to-do list is created correctly, at the end of the day it serves as a scorecard for the previous 24 hours. So often we go through life with no feedback. Are we being a good mom? A good employee? A good business owner? A good human? It's hard to tell.

But when you have your to do list to go by and those checks or strikethroughs marking off the things you've completed, you can pat yourself on the back and rest your head on the pillow knowing that you did what you were supposed to do. (Secret: don't tell, but I sometimes go back and look through old to do lists just as a way to encourage myself and let myself know I'm not just taking up oxygen on this planet. I'm actually getting big stuff done – and I have proof!)

The fourth reason might be the most important to you. Quite simply, to-do lists work. If you follow my process for creating and using your own personal to-do list, you will get more done than you ever thought possible. You'll be focused, productive, and effective, the most powerful trio since Crosby, Stills and Nash cut their last album.

Chapter 3: How To Create To-Do Lists That Get Results

The goal of a to-do list is to get things done. Oddly enough, many people spend more time planning things than they do taking action.

It's important to heed this advice because it's easy to spend too much time planning out your day and not enough time doing things. That's why, in this section, we'll tie everything together into a simple action plan that focuses on helping you get results.

Action 1: Pick a To-Do List Platform

You have two basic choices when it comes to managing your to-do lists:

*1. The paper approach with hard copies kept in a folder.

*2. Digital to-do lists that sync between your desktop and mobile device (like the Remember the Milk app.)

The choice really is up to you. I prefer the paper approach because I like having a binder that's full of my projects and future tasks open wherever I'm working. On the other hand, you might like the syncing, multi-platform capability of a digital to-do list. Regardless of your choice, you need to fully commit to this platform and use it on a daily basis.

Action 2: Use Evernote to Capture Ideas

Evernote is one of the few productivity apps that I use on a regular basis. Odds are, you're constantly bombarded with ideas. The trick is to create a mechanism where you can follow up on a regular basis. With Evernote, you can record ideas and reminders throughout the day, then clip important articles while working on a computer. All can be stored in a central location for easy retrieval.

Action 3: Create Personal and Professional Project Lists

Any task that requires multiple steps should be put into a project list. This will be kept either in a physical folder or in your digital to-do list.

Action 4: Do a Weekly Review

Set aside an hour every week to plan out the next seven days. I prefer Sundays because I'm relaxed from the weekend and energized to tackle the week ahead.

Focus on completing a few actions during this session:

- **Identify appointments and routine tasks.** It's better to know ahead of time if your week is full of appointments and meetings. That way you won't try to cram it full of too many activities. Doing so will only leave you feeling frustrated and unproductive. These prior commitments should be scheduled into your weekly to-do list before your project tasks.

- **Schedule project tasks.** Identify key projects for the next seven days. Then schedule in blocks of time where you can work on specific tasks. Put these into your weekly to-do list and treat them like priority appointments.

- **Identify required energy levels.** Write down a number—from 1 (low) to 5 (high)—next to each task on the weekly to-do list. This rating should match the energy level required to complete the task. Arrange the tasks so they match your personal circadian rhythms.

- **Process captured ideas.** Go through all your notes (from Evernote or the 43 Folders system). Create a short project list for what you'll do for each idea, or schedule a time to follow up on it. This is important because you'll never miss out on a potential opportunity.

That's it!

After completing this weekly review, you'll have a framework that will act as a rough action plan for the next seven days. Just remember to add some flexibility because you never know when an emergency will force you to switch up your schedule.

Action 5: Begin Each Day with MITs

Using your weekly to-do list as a guideline, identify the three tasks that will have the biggest impact on your life. Write them down on a Post-It note or small index card. Then start every day by completing these tasks before anything else. These should be clearly defined actions with specific starting and stopping points. More importantly, pick a metric that measures the successful completion of each task.

Also, plan to take breaks between tasks. Use this time to relax, stretch, walk around or get a cup of coffee. This is important because it recharges your batteries before you focus on the next task.

Action 6: Just Do It!

This step is often the hardest for people. We all have those initial feelings of inertia before starting the workday. The solution? Simply focus on taking that first step and getting started. Here are a few ideas that can help:

- **Remove distractions.** These include dinging and ringing technology like email, social media, instant messages, text messages and phone calls. Distractions can also take the form of desktop clutter, background noise and multitasking. You want to start the day by focusing completely on the most important task.

- **Make preparations.** It's easy to put off tasks if we're not fully prepared to complete them. If you don't have the documents, email messages or software programs you need, you'll waste precious time looking for them. The key to overcoming this problem is to prepare everything ahead of time (like the day before) so you can immediately jump into the task.

- **Commit to getting started.** Stop thinking about how much work it takes to complete a particular task. Instead, focus on completing a really small goal or milestone. This uses the psychology of the mini habits concept I mentioned before— once you get started with a task, momentum usually kicks in and you'll keep going.

- **Focus on "The Now."** Stop agonizing over the many things that need to be completed by the end of the day. Don't worry about failure or what might happen. Simply concentrate on doing the best possible work you can in the time allotted for the task.

- Create a plan for obstacles. Take a few minutes to write down what's going through your mind whenever you get stuck. Is the task too complex to complete? Are you uncertain about how to do something? Do you have a fear of failure? The simplest way to overcome an obstacle is to identify the exact reason you're stuck and work on a plan to get past it.

- Understand the rewards. When all else fails, remind yourself of the long-term value of what completing this task means to you. The more you can tie actions to an important goal, the more motivated you'll feel to take consistent action.

Many people struggle with developing the "getting started habit." My suggestion? Start each day by removing every possible distraction, then focus on completing a series of important tasks to build positive momentum throughout the day.

Action 7: Complete Daily Activities and Appointments

Depending on your schedule, you'll also need to complete daily activities. My advice is to create a list of priorities. Start each day with your top MITs, then work on the items that are almost as important. Keep doing this until you end the day with the tasks that should be done but aren't life or death if they're not completed.

As an example, social media is important for my business, but I also leave it as an "end-of-the-day activity" because it's not as important as writing, creating content and responding to emails from customers.

Action 8: Make Hard Decisions

If an item stays on your list for more than three days, then it's important to do one of three things:

*1. Start the next day by doing it immediately before you do anything else.

*2. Schedule a date in your calendar to take action on it.

*3. Delete it if it's no longer relevant.

One of the problems people have with their to-do lists is they constantly keep adding tasks without eliminating stale ideas. The end result is that they experience guilt because they haven't taken action on tasks that are months old.

Fortunately, there is a simple (but difficult) solution to this problem: Make hard decisions about each task on your list. If you keep putting something off, then you need to immediately take action on it or get rid of it. This shouldn't be a stressful activity. Figure out why you've put off some tasks on your list instead of ignoring them.

Action 9: Practice Continuous Improvement

No to-do list process is perfect from the start. Honestly, I'm still fine-tuning the way I approach my personal productivity. You may find that some of the information in this book isn't relevant to your life. My recommendation? Take what's personally useful and ditch the rest.

At the end the day, the to-do list system you end up using should match what you do on a daily basis. The key here is to test different time management strategies, learn from your experiences every day and keep tweaking the process.

Chapter 4: Popular To-Do List Systems

Task + starting date + closing due date

Even if external circumstances haven't set a deadline, you need to set a self-imposed deadline for each task you work on to make the task easier in your mind and to increase probability that the task will be accomplished on time.

Master list + daily list

We all have tasks that require daily effort. These aren't part of a one-time project. Instead, they're activities that need to be completed on a regular basis. Examples include processing email, making phone calls and running errands. You also have to contend with random meetings, appointments and personal obligations. All of these items should go into a document called a "weekly task list."

Routine tasks make up the bulk of your day, so it's important to plan for them and add them to your calendar. However, it's important not to fall into the trap of blocking out every minute of your day. This habit will turn your weekly list into a grueling regimen that creates unnecessary stress.

My advice is to write down three types of items on a weekly task list: routine tasks that need reinforcement—like new habits;

scheduled appointments, meetings and personal obligations; and important tasks pulled from your project lists.

1 – 3 – 5 rules

The 1-3-5 rule, allows you to tackle nine items in a day. This strategy allows you to take all of the tasks you need done and split them up. You can then start with 1-larger project, then proceed to do the next 3-medium-sized tasks and, finally, complete with the last 5-small stragglers. If you're able to nail everything in your 1-3-5 list in a day, wind down by prepping your 1-3-5 for tomorrow.

Kanban method

All projects are nothing but an accumulation of a large number of smaller processes adding up to bigger ones which in turn add to a larger one and so on. Some of these processes are quick and easy while some are complex and consume time. Executing these processes in a definite sequence is the aim of any project, as we all know.

Kanban is an approach to managing, defining, and enhancing the execution of these processes which leads to efficient release of work. Kanban is a catalyst for organizations and promotes quick and more focused change within. The ease with which change is handled minimizes resistance and adds more value to the organization overall and enables successful execution. After all, the ability to adapt to change is essential to an organization's success.

The Kanban method focuses on creating visibility on what may otherwise be considered as intangible knowledge work. The whole purpose of this is to ensure that the entire service functions on the correct amount of work. The point is that there should be no work requested by the customer that should not be delivered. Essentially, a Kanban system is a delivery flow system which reduces the work in progress (WIP) via the use of visual signals.

Other to-do list methods are:

- Massive, all-inclusive list
- 3+2 strategy
- Project based system
- Matrix system
- Getting things done

Chapter 5: First Things First

Now that you know the power of the to-do list, you're probably raring to go jump into a makeover of your own list. But let's pull the camera back a bit before we go into the day-to-day. In order for our to-do lists to move us in the right direction, we have to know what the right direction is!

Look around where you are right now. Whether you're in your bedroom (like I am) or at the office or at the local Starbucks, you can probably see a million calls for your attention, right now. As I scan my bedroom, I see laundry that needs to be folded (always!), my nephew's computer and school books that need to be put away, a stack of books to read, and dogs to walk, hand weights to lift, and Facebook – always Facebook!

So how is it possible to know what the right things are at any point in time? Well, we have to start at the top; we start with our priorities – our dreams, our "grand visions," as I call them. We have to start with exactly what you want your future to look like, in Technicolor, complete with Dolby surround sound and 3D.

It's popular these days to select a word for the year, or create an intention like "beauty," "grace," or "fly." If you've fallen into this trend, it feels really good to pick a word that you want to represent your year. Maybe you get a necklace engraved, and you might paint it on your wall, and you excitedly tell others about what you're intending for the upcoming 12 months, but often that's where it ends.

After all, how do you bring "fly" or "breathe" out of the ether into the everyday? How do you make it something you can DO? It's difficult, which is why we often lose touch with our word (or our resolutions) somewhere around springtime.

But never fear. I have an alternative to the ephemeral. I'm going to help you create goals and dreams that are actually DO-ABLE, but first let's talk about priorities. You probably know by now that I'm a word nerd, so I like to start with the definition.

I love that priorities are things that are TREATED as more important, not just things that we SAY are more important. 2

When we start talking about priorities, the ones that come up most often are those I call "The Five Fs:"

- Faith

- Family

- Friends

- Fitness

• Finances

Other common values include community, creativity, leadership, relationships, authenticity, and more.

These are all great words... but how do you take, say, "relationships," and put it on your to-do list? There's nothing to do, and as we've discussed, that's what a to-do list IS – things you can DO. And that right there is the big disconnect between dreams and intentions and the everyday.

We often know what we want in a fuzzy, feel-good, long-term sense, but we don't know what to do TODAY to get there. We have an intuitive sense of what our priorities or "one word" means, but we don't make sure we know exactly what we want. And if we get to the point where we can say that our priority is "relationships," we're still not sure where we're headed because, even though we know that "relationships" are important to us, there are a million different types of relationships. There are even a million types of GOOD relationships!

As a result, it becomes frustrating and difficult to work today towards this dream for tomorrow. So March or April comes and we set our dreams and intentions aside, and we go back to folding laundry and answering the stuff at the top of the email in-box. After all, there's plenty of that to keep us busy.

If you're tired of living that way, of trying hard but not making the progress you long to, then let's keep going. It's time to take the first step to rocking your to-do list by determining your priorities.

TASK: Take five minutes to write down your top three to five priorities. Don't worry about the order (if "health" comes before or after "faith," for instance). Don't worry about if you're getting them all down; this is just a starting point.

Don't worry if your priorities are different than they were a year or two ago. At different periods in our life things might move up and down the priority list. You are not static – your life changes, your priorities change. That's GOOD. Just think about right here and now, and what your priorities are today. This is just a snapshot in time, so don't let it stress you out. I'm teaching you a process, something you can go back to again and again.

Remember, there are no "right" or "wrong" priorities; they are uniquely yours and require no defense or explanation.

Chapter 6: Planning is Key: Keep Lists and Use the Tools At Your Disposal

A wise man once said that the plan is nothing, but planning is everything. We all have big plans about something. It's a great way to gain some perspective of your life's objectives. But what many of us don't realize is that you need to determine the path of the plan, otherwise it may become a pretty picture to look at, something forgotten in the back of your mind.

Keeping lists is the best way to stay on the right track. The path to a certain goal may seem clear at the time, but suddenly you see yourself in the middle of the plan, jam-packed with paperwork, additional work and people asking you question, that require time and further effort on your part. All these obstacles can give you headaches and distract you from your goal.

Start making lists. Not just to-do lists – all types of lists. Your diary is a type of list keeping habit, so is the grocery list on your refrigerator. You know how handy your diary is when you are trying to remember when the last fight with your friend was, so let's show you different types of lists, so you can decide which will become your lifesaver:

Shopping Lists – these are necessary in every household. You will want to write down everything you need to buy the moment you take the last out of the refrigerator. Have a board in your kitchen, to pin stickers on, or keep them in a pile on the fridge itself. In time, you will know which products you need to buy weekly and which are your monthly purchases. You can make tables on the computer, containing the products you buy weekly, and just add the new products under the weekly ones.

Another stressful and time-consuming hassle we often encounter is gift shopping. Christmas, Mother's Day, Father's Day, you name it. Who's to say you can't plan gifts in advance. Keep your notebook handy in case you come across something you think someone if your life might like. You may not remember all the gift ideas you've bumped into throughout the year, so when a big event like New Year's or a birthday comes along, you can just take your notebook out and use is as a cheat sheet.

Check Lists – these types of lists are convenient when you have to arrive prepared to a meeting or event. Stress can often make you forget, so keep a record of the essential things you need for a certain interaction or occasion. Let's say you have a presentation. Your list should include all the things you need to make it successful. These things may include:

- Copies of the project's outline

- Model of the product

- Laptop, slides, projector and etc.

- Spare battery or a power cable

- Pens: red, blue, black

- Lucky charm

Resource Lists – if you find a source of information to be statistically accurate and in accordance to your requirements, keep it categorized. We live in the new century, so take advantage of the tools at our disposal. You can create several folders in your browser, all titled differently (e.g. recipes, news, fun, movies and etc.) so you can speed up the search when you most need it.

Many browsers have the option to create several users. You can name one "Work", for when you're working; another one titled "Home", for when you're surfing for fun; and of course, you can open a different user for each person in your household that uses the same computer, so your browsing history and analytics don't intersect.

It will be of great benefit if you open a Google email account just for work. That way, when your boss needs a log of your working activities or asks a question about the source of the information, you can just log in to your account and search for the sources you used. If you are the boss, ask all your employees to use the email address you provided, so you can keep track of their performance.

List of Ideas – we come up with ideas throughout the whole day, but usually remember one or two, or none, in some cases. There are many times when you encounter a situation that inspires you to try a different course of action. Sometimes it may be an idea to check out some detail from a different perspective, or the word you were looking for just popped up in your head when you were washing your hands in the toilet. Write this little stuff in a notebook and look over the list daily.

Money Lists – this is a tough one, especially if you lack organizational skills. Keeping a list, where all your expenses will be recorded, will give you a sound evidence of where your money goes. To do this successfully, keep the receipts of everything you buy. If you forgot your receipt, write the item down on your phone or a notebook. At the end of the month, when you calculate the totals, you will see how much you spend on food, bills, leisure and taxes. In time, you will learn what is necessary and what can be left out. These types of lists shift the focus on the big picture and will give you an idea where and how you can cut back.

Lists for goals – these are the most complex lists and call for special attention. You will need to go over each separately, and calculate the time and means you will need to achieve them. Having a goal and building a plan to get to it, will motivate you and activate all your capabilities. Without one, you may end up squandering your efforts and time, to build someone else's dreams and achievements.

According to the Zeigarnik Effect, human beings tend to remember the stuff they didn't do more than the stuff they already completed. That's why it will be best to keep a notebook ready in your phone or purse, for both the stuff you already did and the details you believe you might forget later. The first one will help you to keep track of your achieved goals. As the Zeigarnik effect implies, we often forget the tasks we finished, so it will be a nice reminder of everything you've completed throughout the day or week. Some days are so busy, you are not sure if your head is still on your shoulders, yet you feel like you haven't accomplished anything. Keep your finished tasks listed and you'll be surprised how much work you are actually capable of.

Many tools are available if you only make the effort to plan ahead. From the old-school pen and notebook record keeping, to advanced mobile applications to make your life a lot easier. There is even a specially designed device for making lists and keeping contacts on the go, called a personal digital assistant or PDA. Nowadays it's not very popular, because mobile phones are capable of supporting much more advanced applications.

Today's applications and virtual assistants have many options. You can assign different colors to each type of task in the calendar, so you can find them without having to read each. For example, assign red for meetings, green for events, blue for making phone calls or sending emails. The application might be capable of grouping different types of tasks by priority, category or date. Most have the option to remind you before a task and you can assign the actual time when the application will remind you, e.g. 3 hours before the deadline, a day, a week and etc. Best of all, today's devices have access to the internet, so don't forget to use Google Drive, Dropbox and similar platforms to store and share files, documents and photos whenever you need to.

It will be smart to make all types of lists and use several types of assistants. Download a virtual assistant for your to-do lists throughout the day and tasks related to the job. Have a notebook in your purse or pocket for the small things you come up with during the day. Put up a board next to your fridge and keep track of the spent items. Use the recording option on your phone to list the things you can't write down at the moment. We don't count those few seconds while we write something down, but when the time comes, you will realize that you saved valuable time, a time you can spend enjoying your life more.

Chapter 7: When to Work on Routine Tasks
(Like Email)

Email is an ongoing thing. The problem with stopping every five minutes to answer email is that the time you use is digging into time that you should be spending on more productive activities. Yes, of course, you do need to answer your email in a fairly timely manner, but you don't need to keep breaking off from your target work on your to-do list to do this. Those that do will find that they really do make a mess of things and are not that productive because they are too easily sidetracked. So you need to set a specified time that you'll check and respond to emails each day.

You need to learn to use your email in the best possible way. If you allot yourself a certain amount of time for email, what you can do is set up an automatic answering system so that people know you'll follow up when you have time. You can change the message regularly and that's pretty easy to do and only takes seconds, but if they get a reply from you, at least they will be happy. The kind of wording I use in mine is standard and I keep a standard Word document with all the wording so I don't have to type it out each time:

Thank you for your email. Please note I am currently busy at this time, but I will get back to you very soon.

That's a standard one, but you can add to it or make it more specific if you have a set time of day that you answer your emails:

Thank you for your email. I check my emails daily around 10 a.m. and I will be replying to your email then. If, in the meantime, this is something of an urgent nature, you can of course contact me through my mobile number.

The idea of these notes is to make sure that your clients know that their email has been received. Then, you need to decide how to fit time into your day to deal with emails without distraction so that you can get through them quickly and empty the inbox. Remember that multi-tasking is not going to help you when you have jobs to do. Thus, put aside half an hour twice a day for emails. This could be first thing in the morning when you arrive at the office and when you come back from lunch.

Then go through the email and browse at each to see the level of urgency of the email. Some will be things that you can answer relatively quickly without too much thought and that will whittle the amount of emails that you have down, once you have dealt with these. Then deal with those for which you have answers and can deal with without having to leave your desk to get more information. Lastly, deal with the lengthy emails or the emails that may require you to do a little more scouting around before you can answer them. You do need to make sure that your filing system for emails is a good one, so that you have information at the tips of your fingers. It's no good going through 5000 emails trying to find that one that gives you the information that you need. If you sort them into separate boxes, you will know where to find them and that saves you oodles of time.

To save you a lot of time, there are certain things that you can do. For example, the greeting at the top of the email is almost standard. If you keep note of the kind of things that you say, you can have one file with standard email templates and if you have an email system such as CRM, you are able to put the template in when you reply to the email. If you don't have a CRM then you can keep a separate file with all of this information but do make sure that you set up your email so that your professional signature is already in it because this will save you a lot of time too.

Routine bulk shouldn't take you that long if you get yourself organized. In business, if you don't know the answer to someone's problem, don't waste time writing back to them and saying:

I am not sure. I will have to check into it and get back to you.

It's not the most professional of answers. It's far better that you refer to a colleague who can answer their query and write back to the client as follows:

Your email has been passed to my colleague, ..., who will be able to get back to you very soon. For your information, his email address is ....

By doing this, you are taking this off your to-do list, or in fact it is never going to hit your to-do list. Your colleague can take over and your job is finished on this item, leaving nothing outstanding.

That's a much more sensible way of dealing with email and it means that you have not wasted time on things that you don't know the answers to. The amount of time that is wasted scouting around for answers is an awful lot. Once you sit down to answer your emails, answer them. Do not talk on IM. Don't put any of them off until later as later doesn't always come and set up your automatic replies so that they will last until such time as you are back in your seat answering email again.

This gives you much peace of mind because you know that you have dealt with everything that has come in and that all of those who write to you following that session will have a reply even if just tells them to wait. It's better than no acknowledgement at all and it keeps everyone happy.

Other routine tasks

Email will not be the only routine task that you have to deal with and if you can sort your post into priority piles this helps as well. When you are dealing with paperwork, it's best to have a pile that is easily dealt with, that which requires input from others and that which is urgent. Deal with the urgent stuff first thing in the morning and then if you have time to spare after your emails are done, plow into the pile of stuff that is easy to deal with because you can make your pile much more manageable. If there are items of paperwork or posts that need other input from others, then use your camera on your phone and send it to them. That takes seconds. You can also mark it to say that you did that and follow up later on. That way, all you are left with is the stuff that really does need your attention that is fairly easy to get through when you are energized. Thus, after a break or after your meal is the ideal time. By the end of the day, your paperwork and your emails should all have been dealt with, so that you have a clear desk ready for the morning, and anything which was not dealt with needs to be put on your calendar with an alert so that you can integrate it into your to-do list for the following day.

Chapter 8: Using Your To-Do List to Set Goals and Deadlines

Why should you set goals and deadlines? How will this benefit you? A goal is something that you want to achieve in the future. It can be a short or long term and can be as simple as wanting to get to work on time. If you don't have a goal of something that you want to achieve, you won't ever get anywhere. It won't matter to you if you get to work 10 minutes late or 30 minutes late. You'll continue to aimlessly go through life. On the other hand, if you establish goals that you want to achieve and a time period in which you want to complete the goal, you'll have a sense of purpose throughout your day. This sense of purpose will encourage you to set more and more goals as you experience the accomplishment of successfully completing the items on your to-do list.

Using your to-do list to set goals and deadlines is a helpful way to break larger goals into manageable action items. There are many things in your life that can't be accomplished within a single day if you're a normal person, let alone a working mother. There are some days that you can't put down write the bills and update the checkbook on a one day to-do list. You may need to put write out the bills on the first day. The second day may need to be document receipts into the checkbook. And, the third day may have to be update the checkbook balance. It all depends on what other activities that you know you have to get done that day and knowing your time limitations. If you also have a school activity on the night that your planning to complete the bills, don't set yourself up for failure. Multiple failures begin to eat at your self-esteem and can cause you to give up on goal setting. Don't forgo sleep. A lack of sleep will jeopardize all of your goals for the next day, which would lead to a vicious cycle of failure and crankiness.

Additionally, there are goals that can't be completed in one day. You can't put finish your degree on a one day to-do list. Unless it happens to be the day of the graduation and all you have to do is wait at home to get your diploma. But even then, you can't control when the diploma will arrive in the mail. If you want actual proof that you completed your degree that day, you would have to go to the ceremony which would require several action items to be completed before you're able to walk across the stage and receive the certificate.

Even a much smaller project such as cleaning my basement in comparison to you finishing your degree might not be able to be completed in a day. If I don't have a vacation day, the kids will be home in the evening, and I value sleep (ah, I do miss sleep), it's likely impossible to complete such a daunting task without breaking it into manageable steps. Some of you might think this is an exaggeration. You haven't seen my basement! Two storage lockers shoved into an 1800 square feet basement full of half opened boxes with their contents spilling onto the dusty floor.

Your first step is to identify the goal that you would like to accomplish. Once the goal has been established, break that goal down into actionable steps that you'll need to complete in order to reach the goal. If it's a long-range type of goal, even those actionable steps will need to be broken down into multiple smaller steps. Once you have all of those items broken down, you'll be able to identify what you can accomplish on a daily basis to achieve that goal in the future. Each item marked off of your to-do list will bring you one step closer to your ultimate goal.

Breaking your goals down into daily achievable tasks will help you not to give up on the goal before you even give yourself the chance to succeed.

Key Take Always:

- There are goals that can't be completed in one day. Using your to-do list to set goals and deadlines is a helpful way to break larger goals into manageable action items.

- Once you've identified a goal that you want to accomplish, break that goal down into actionable steps that you will need to complete in order to reach that goal.

- On a daily basis, identify one thing that you can accomplish which will assist you in achieving that goal in the future.

Chapter 9: Define Goals and Motivation

It is impossible to change and manage time better without personal goals to accomplish the change. If your habits annoy your boss, your spouse, or your friends – that isn't enough.

What do you hope to get out of better organization: more money, more recognition in your career, or among friends or simply, better quality of life?

Any of the above desires, along with countless others, can be sufficient to drive a person to make significant changes to their productivity and organization. However, that is the requirement: goals for you and you alone.

SMART goals

Now that you have found your why for attempting the mastery of to-do lists, and with those to-do lists your life as a whole, you can begin to strive for SMART goals. Yes, this means goals that are wise to aim for, but it also has a very significant meaning to attribute to each goal you set.

These goals are:

· Specific – The Five W's come into play here. Make sure for the goal you can answer Who, What, When, Where, and Why.

· Measurable – Set a way ahead of time to determine if you are meeting your goals, a specific "yardstick" if you will, to measure if you have done what you hoped to do.

· Attainable – With your schedule, and all the different aspects of your life, can you see yourself accomplishing this? If not, it's time to re-draft.

· Relevant – Goals you set are for your benefit. Therefore, don't seek to win an award in an area you aren't interested in just to impress someone. Do things you can be proud of and set goals accordingly.

· Timely - A time frame for completion and the ability to say, "Yes, I definitely accomplished that goal," are necessary here.

Another way to define goals, introduced in the book, Made to Stick by Chip Heath & Dan Heath, is SUCCES, also known as sticky goals. These goals are:

· Simple – The basic idea is easily shared.

- Unexpected – Out of the ordinary or not "the norm."

- Concrete – Ideas with numerous details usually stick the best. Stories passed through generations are good examples.

- Credible – You could believe it happened to someone else.

- Emotional Stories – You empathize with the individuals in the story.

Now you are asking, how does this set of criteria apply to your to-do list goals? It is as basic as this: these types of goals grab your attention. Obviously, emailing the team does not grab your attention and interest like creating a new piece of art or an ad campaign for a cause you believe in. So, create your goals with these criteria in mind, but not a must on every goal. This adds a level of newness to your thinking and can help you become more well-rounded if nothing else.

It is important to break a large goal into smaller goals. This is easier to measure and schedule so you can watch yourself work toward that large goal. Having the large goal with no measurable steps toward attainment makes distraction and procrastination that much easier.

Having smaller steps toward the final deadline makes it easier to take breaks to recharge your batteries or to get small rewards en route to the big payoff.

What's holding you back

It's time to address the items that interfere with your level of production. First, make a list of things most commonly get in the way when you are attempting to cross items off your to-do list. If you are just beginning to implement to-do lists, make a list of things that distract you two or more days a week on a regular basis.

Distractions can take up as much as two hours of your day. This means a significant dent in the total time set aside to be effective.

At two hours per day, seven days per week and 52 weeks per year, you spend an average of 57,512 hours distracted (based on an average U.S. Lifespan of 79 years). Obviously, with some effort, at least a portion of that time can be put to much better use.

One of the biggest factors that impedes, distracts, and prevents successful time management today is social media. Having instant access to other members of the team through various forms of communication can be beneficial. The ability to research on the run is obviously much better than being stuck in a library for hours or days just to find the idea you are researching falls flat. However, the downside of these obvious benefits is the access to things you could be living without.

There is no reason to check in with friends or old high school buddies on a daily basis on Facebook. There is no absolute need to know instantaneously via notification or email that you received an invitation to a game on any number of social media platforms.

Finally, to be honest, not everyone needs to be able to check their email every few minutes. Yes, some important business deals are accomplished by sending documents via email. It is true that negotiations can be done via email as well. However, for the majority of us, checking email every two minutes or with every harmonious ding is simply detracting from the momentum we could have toward the completion of the project before us or the idea that is slowly coming into being during a brainstorming session.

Natural Tendencies vs. "The Way Everyone Does It"

Have you noticed you accomplish things more easily in the morning or the evening? Set aside time for these tasks when you are most likely to be successful in their completion. Not everyone is made for a 9 to 5 workday or even success during daylight hours. If you tend to find more creativity or more ambition in the afternoon or evening, don't try to force yourself to work harder in the morning. Things will not work out in your favor.

Instead, make sure to organize your schedule in such a way that you will reach success. If you know you start out slow in the morning but tend to hit the ground running after lunch, make your to-do list with easier tasks for morning hours and the bulk of your jobs set for afternoon completion.

Finding personal strengths is important for many reasons in life. Knowing what you are most excited about and particularly talented in paves the way to success as much as being organized and productive. Think outside the box to determine the best ways for you to approach a task or the areas of the task you know you do best. The next step is making sure to always put more weight on the things you are good at in a situation but allow more time for the areas that you recognize as outside your talent area.

Chapter 10: Time Management

What is time management and how can it be used to drive you into action, productivity, self-discipline, and success? Let's tell you a story to illustrate the concept of time management compellingly.

A professor brought three different trays of pebbles, large rocks, and sand to the class. He asks a student volunteer to empty all three trays in a bucket. A student walks up to the front of the class and starts performing the task diligently. He begins with the sand, followed by pebbles and finally attempts to empty the rocks. However, much to his dismay, he is unable to fit it all in the bucket.

The professor then turned to the class and announced that it only the student has filled the bucket with rocks first and later by pebbles and finally sand, he would've been able to fit everything in.

This is precisely how time management works. It is about organizing your rocks, pebbles, and sand to fit it all in a limited bucket of 24 hours a day. Focus on tackling the most challenging and biggest tasks first, followed by the medium-sized and smallest ones. When we focus on smaller tasks first, there is a tendency to spend more time obsessing about it than required. In our zest for over perfection and over-analysis, we may spend more time than required on it. This leaves little time for mid-sized and bigger tasks.

In essence, the concept of time management is about organizing, scheduling and planning your available time resources to achieve maximum productivity. If you don't reserve enough time for the big rocks, the pebbles and sand will occupy all your time.

Time is true wealth because once gone it can never return. You can't turn back time however much you want to change something. Everyone has the same 24 hours in a day (unless you have access to some secret gadget or superpower). Yet, some people manage to do a lot with their time, while others complain they never have time for anything.

How is it that some people always have the time to finish their task on time while others are struggling to find time to balance work and leisure activities? How is it that some people not just complete their tasks on time but also enjoy their hobbies while others are barely able to honor deadlines?

How are some folks always working ahead of their schedule while other people run around like headless chickens trying to finish tasks at the last moment? It is all about time management. How you utilize the available 24 hours can make all the difference to your productivity and efficiency.

Here are some of the best time management techniques that can get your productivity to skyrocket.

1. Create a morning routine. This isn't an exaggeration but the manner in which you begin your day will determine to a large extent how productive or valuable you will be throughout the day. It will establish or set the momentum for how much you will manage to pack into the day.

Avoid snoozing. Much as you are tempted to hit the snooze button and grab a few extra minutes of sleep, get up and going. Staying in bed will make you feel more lethargic and drowsy, not to mention you may just end up falling asleep all over again. It will be harder to awaken once the alarm goes off.

Start with some exercises to feel refreshed and rejuvenated. It will jumpstart your brain activity region and boost metabolism. Even a short run or on the spot exercises can be helpful. Make the most of your morning routine to set the pace for your entire day. I'd highly recommend arising before other people in the house wake up. This can be your best and most productive time to get things done.

This is also a good time to plan your day's activities or practice yoga/meditation. Reply to emails or create a plan of action for the day before it begins. If you are pressed for time and have plenty of things lined up for the day, get organized. Make a well-planned and organized list by focusing your efforts and energy on high priority and urgent tasks for the day. Identify important tasks from errands, and schedule the latter around the former.

Identify the three most important things that need to be done during the day. What are the things you really want to get done by the end of the day? Make these tasks your priority. Everything else can wait. Don't try to fit in more than you can handle throughout the day. You will be stunned by how much progress you'll make with your time management simply by following this one tip.

2. Recognize and discard time suckers. Do this quick exercise to gauge where a majority of your time is being spent. I called it a daily time audit. Do a seven-day audit of where you are spending your time. Record everything on a phone, notebook or journal. What are you doing right now? Break it into blocks 30 or 60 minutes. Did you manage to get plenty of things done today? Was your time effectively invested?

Did you waste time or unproductive activities? If you are using the four-quadrant technique, categorize your activities based on the four quadrants. At the end of each week, tally all your numbers. Where did you spend a major chunk of your time? Which quadrant did a majority of your activities fit in? The results may stun you! At times, we believe we are being productive when we are clearly not. We live under the illusion that we are getting a lot then owing to multitasking. However, our brain power and efficiency take a hit when we do too many things at a time. Are you accomplishing the desired productivity and efficiency or simply taking on plenty of things to do.

Bad habits are the biggest time wasters created only to reduce productivity. The most devastating thing about these time wasters is that they give us a sense of accomplishing a lot. For instance, we may keep surfing the net for hours telling ourselves we are researching or hunting for ideas. Can you imagine the wasteful utilization of time by being on Instagram, Facebook or Pinterest for hours trying to gather ideas? Instead, do a quick browse through and get back to work.

Add a timer if required. I find this works well for me. Each time I am tempted to research or find ideas on the internet in the middle of my work hours, I time my internet and social media browsing. Set a timer for the next 5-10 minutes. Once it buzzes, you are snapped out of your browsing or ideating time and back to work. Similarly, time yourself when it comes to chatting on the phone.

One of the biggest time wasters I've realized is checking and replying to emails throughout the day. Our mailbox keeps buzzing throughout the day and we are tempted to check and reply to every damn email in the middle of something else, thus killing the momentum of the current task at hand. Avoid doing this. Instead, reserve a time for checking and replying to your emails (unless it is absolutely urgent). Keep asking yourself whether what you are spending time on is adding any real value to your overall tasks or productivity.

Browsing social media, playing mindless virtual games, binge-watching series and so on are all time wasters and negative habits that sap your time and efficiency. Use your time well if you want to accomplish your objectives. The fundamental difference between losers and winners is that the latter are able to delay gratification and concentrate on what needs to be done while having their vision firmly fixated on the bigger picture. They are focused on long term rewards, which drive them to their goals via optimal utilization of valuable time resources. You will seldom find them focusing on instant pleasures.

We all envy the rich and successful, yet we cannot get ourselves to undergo their struggle or undergo the challenges they go through or the sacrifices they make to attain a certain level of life success. Among other things that contribute to their success, there is time management, delayed gratification, self-discipline, the ability to overcome procrastination and much more. We wonder why we aren't as successful or the people we admire. Are you prepared to give up your time wasters and bad habits? Are you prepared to delay gratification like them? Are you prepared to become productive and hustle each day to make the most of your valuable time resources? Do you have it in you to delay short term gratification for long term success? Use your time resources smartly if you truly want to be successful.

You are not getting much done by watching Netflix for hours or play virtual games unless you are a scriptwriter/movie maker or virtual games creator/writer. Channelize each minute towards optimizing your productivity. This may fast-track your way to success. Yes, there's no denying that things can get a bit overwhelming at times. When you begin to feel a sense of being overwhelmed or intimidated by the task at hand, take a short break or power nap. Gather your senses, and get back to the task with renewed energy and enthusiasm.

If you've read author Charles Duhig's book titled The Power of Habit, it talks about keystone habits that weave together all other stones. These keystone habits not just help us develop other productive habits but also help get rid of unproductive habits. By concentrating on keystone habits, we learn to manage our overall time efficiently, which makes creating habits related to time management, procrastination, and productivity much easier.

Train and develop the brain's other side too. For example, spend time learning skills that are beyond your comfort zone or something you'd not expect yourself to do. For example, if you are a doctor, spend some time releasing the stress by learning dance. Similarly, a pianist can learn taekwondo. Spend time on activities that are beyond your comfort zone to train your brain to acquire new skills.

3. Get some inspiration when you are not feeling motivated. Go to YouTube, LinkedIn or Ted Talks each time you find your spirit to do things sagging. These can be excellent resources for getting you back on the inspiration track. It is hard to do things when the drive from within is exhausting. Identify ways to turn on your fire by concentrating on inspiring content, and seeking motivation. Reading about other people's success stories and actions can put you back into action mode by turning on the fire in your belly.

I also like the idea of getting a mentor who can guide you, make you accountable and keep you on track with your tasks. It is pretty easy to get distracted and discouraged when there's no one to guide you. However, when we can rely on someone to guide (who themselves have been through the grind), we tend to become more proactive, accountable and responsible. It always keeps us motivated and inspired to stay on the right track. Find a mentor who can keep you aligned with your tasks and goals.

4. Make the most of your waiting time. Use your waiting time well. We get plenty of waiting time that can be used to boost productivity and make the most of our available time. For example, at the airport, at the coffee shop waiting for our order, at the doctor's, etc. Make the most of this waiting time for doing small tasks like creating a rough outline for a project, brainstorming, ideating, scheduling events for the next day,

sending emails and messages and so on. You can't do many challenging and focus intensive tasks at such a time. So it's best to pick lighter take that can free up a large chunk of your 'doing' time. There's a lot of groundwork you can get done within these small time gaps. And we all know a strong foundation leads to a solid structure.

5. Divide a to-do list of things based on four quadrants. As you complete each task, mark it on the list to give you a sense of accomplishment, success, and fulfillment of completing each task, which will motivate you to take on more tasks.

Use your downtime judiciously. We have plenty of downtime or filler time all through the day that can be used for making your task list. How about utilizing your travel time for planning, scheduling and organizing the entire day's tasks? Commuting time can also be used for listening to audio books or podcasts.

Avoid devoting every waking moment of your free time to organizing and planning the day, which can prove counterproductive to the process of productivity and time management. If you have about 15-20 free minutes, devote five minutes for organizing the day's task.

Make the most of your weekends too. Now I am sounding like a dreaded productivity monster. However, you'll be surprised at how much you can manage to pack in by utilizing your weekends. There is a meme on the social media about a man throwing papers in the air on Friday evening and saying something like, "-- you, its Friday." The next image is of the same man collecting papers thrown on Friday evening on Monday morning. Pretty powerful, if you ask me! Even a little planning and starter work during weekends can help ease the oncoming week's pressure. It can be something as no-fuss as creating a rough draft or planning your week.

Spend about 2-4 hours every day doing productive tasks on a weekend. You'll still be left with lots of time for relaxation and leisure during weekends. Try pushing in tasks during weekends and filler time throughout the day, and notice how much more you will manage to do.

Some of the most successful people plan their entire week a day before the weeks begin. This keeps them focused on their priorities, while smoothly going into the next week. Once you get into a relaxed weekend mode, it's challenging to suddenly shift to a more productive Monday mode. You make the transition less jerky and smoother by beginning on Sunday itself.

Walking into your work week with a clear plan helps you focus on priorities. We can effortlessly transition from a casual and relaxed weekend mindset to an action-oriented Monday morning brain if we keep everything ready the previous on Sunday. Take a few minutes on Sunday to make a plan for the entire week. Eliminate procrastination by breaking down weekly objectives into daily tasks so each time you need to get something done, all you have to do is a glance at your to-do list.

Keep in mind that your energy, enthusiasm, and creativity keep fluctuating through the week. Schedule low effort and priority tasks for Monday and other times when your energy and spirit are relatively low. Similarly, schedule demanding, creative and challenging tasks on Tuesday and Wednesday when your productivity is known to be at its peak. Schedule meetings and brainstorming session on Thursday when the team's doing energy begins declining. Use Fridays for networking, doing a round-up of the week and planning.

6. Create periodic reminders. If you don't want to lag behind your schedule and make the most of your time, set regular reminders, alarms and deadline alerts on your gadgets at frequent intervals instead of the final deadline. Setting reminders at regular intervals for sub-deadlines helps you stay on track with the final deadline, instead of waiting until the last minute.

For instance, if you have a project due to be submitted in the next 4 weeks, set reminders for not just at the end of 28 days but also day 7, 12, 18, 24 and 28. This ensures that you are on track with the tasks required to complete the project. You are periodically reminded on the task, and on track instead of scampering around trying to finish it at the tail end of your deadline.

7. Rise early. Did you know that some of the world's most successful people are part of the 5 a.m. club? And here you are, sleeping away to glory and wondering why you don't manage to accomplish the wealth and success they witness. It's a matter of time management, discipline, and choice. You choose your actions, and they eventually impact your chances of success.

If you ask me my favorite time management technique, it is rising early and starting as soon as possible. It gives you an edge like few other things. Mark Twain's famous quote is worth mentioning here. He said, "If it is your job to eat a frog, it is best to do it first thing in the morning. And if it is your job to eat two frogs, it is best to eat the bigger frog first." This pretty much says it all about ace time management tactics.

If you feel intimidated by the prospect of doing a lot in one day, begin early. Keep everything related to the task ready the previous night so you eliminate time wasters such as trying to figure out where to begin.

For example, lets us say you are working on a crucial report base on facts and statistics you've been accumulating over a while. Ensure all your research is neatly organized in a folder or document for easy access. When you have everything you need to begin, it is easy to get into quick action mode and pick momentum.

However, if you waste time trying to figure out where to begin, you slow down the process of starting and completing the task. In the above example, if all your facts and statistics are easily accessible to you, it is easier to begin.

Similarly, if you have an important presentation or meeting scheduled for the next day, keep your clothes and everything else ready the previous day so you don't waste time or exhaust your energy trying to locate things. A major chunk of our morning time is spent on what to wear and planning our look for the day. If you keep everything ready the previous day, it is easier to focus on the big task.

Also, if you have plenty of things lined up for the day, and they are all crucial, tackle the most challenging task first. The objective is to finish the most time consuming and toughest task (remember the professor's sand, pebbles and rock example?) by noon. Once you complete an overwhelming task, you'll experience a greater sense of accomplishment. This will inspire you to tackle the other tasks with a more go-getter, action-oriented mind frame.

When you know you have plenty to finish the next day or have a long working day ahead, avoid staying up until late. Few things hamper your productivity and time management than lack of sleep. Sleep early, and enjoy uninterrupted sleep for a good 8-9 hour awake fresh and rejuvenated for the day. Lack of sleep can make you irritable, low on energy and unable to focus (low on mental alertness and concentration).

One of the worst things you can do to hit your productivity and time management is to dive into a day with zero ideas about where to get started. Imagine trying to spend half an hour trying to figure out where to begin or what needs to be done through the day when this time could've been used to begin the day's tasks and finish early. Now you'll complete the task late, which doesn't give you much time to plan the next day's activities. You are unknowingly caught in a vicious circle. Avoid flaking from one task to another, and losing time. Plan your day ahead of time to skyrocket your productivity.

Always recommend clearing the work desk the previous day, and making a list of things that need to be completed the next day. It is known as the decompression method. You'll experience a sense of positivity, rejuvenation, and freshness once you walk into a neater, more organized and cleaner looking desk. Arrive a little early to work, and start putting together the work material you need to begin the day with a bang. This one tip can literally be the one thing that impacts your productivity through the day.

8. Leverage time, work and skills. Ever wondered why some people manage to accomplish remarkable results and others simply slog it out even though everyone has the same 24 hours

in a day? It is a lot working smart and making clever utilization of time by leveraging time, effort and skills.

For instance, you have 24 hours a day, out of which only 12-15 hours max can be used for productive pursuits. If you work even for 15 hours a day, five days a week you are clocking productive time worth 75 hours, and probably burning yourself out.

Now contrast this with leveraging other people's time, efforts and skill. You hire 3 people who are each putting in 40 hours of work each week, which makes it 120 hours a week! See the difference? Running a marathon will limit your scope to grow. There's only so much you can accomplish by working alone.

However, if you run a relay, there's a lot you can get done. By leveraging other people' time, effort and energy, you aren't burning yourself out. Everyone is pitching in a little to contribute to overall productivity instead of one person trying to do everything. Most successful people around the world realize the value of leveraging time, skills and effort. They build empires out of other people's time, efforts and skills.

Delegate and outsource time-consuming tasks. Remember Pareto's 80-20 rule? Only 20 percent of efforts are contributing to 80 percent of your results. Why would you spend the other 80 percent of your time doing something else? Wouldn't you want to increase your results by investing more time in what is clearly working for you? Delegate tasks and responsibilities that are occupying a major chunk of your time. It can tricky in the beginning to get someone else to do your work. However, if you don't train people and delegate responsibilities, you will be running the marathon alone, and pretty much limiting your results. Delegating tasks and outsourcing can be smart time savers. It reduces your workload and allows you to focus on tasks that are bringing results. Plus by hyper-focusing on a task, you are preventing your brain from slowing down. We know by now, multitasking is a bad idea. For increasing productivity and making yourself more efficient, spend more time on tasks that get you results while delegating time-consuming tasks to others. You can either give responsibilities to team members by training and guiding them or hire qualified and experienced freelancers. Hiring people in the house may take initial investment and training but it can be worth it in the long haul.

9. Make a routine. This one seems like a no-brainer to me yet it is funny how many people don't do it. You are likelier to make the most of your time by sticking to a clear routine. If there isn't a fixed time scheduled for activities during the day, you'll end up wasting a lot of time by having little control of your time. Set a clear time schedule for activities throughout the day. This will ensure you pull out all stops to get things done. Schedule each day as if you are planning an important event.

These are some of the best time management secrets to get you into productivity overdrive, minimize wastage of time, organize available time resources and snap you out of snooze mode.

Chapter 11: Correlation of Time Management Skills and Success

As we begin this chapter, let me caution you. I'm sure that we have all heard the different clichés about putting ourselves in other's shoes. This is a time when that shouldn't be done. Don't look at someone who appears successful and says that you want to be that person. You don't know what that person sacrificed in order to have such success. That person may look at you and say how he wishes that he had a family. So, are we clear? Only look at yourself and what you wish to have based on your priorities and wants.

What is success anyway? The definition of success depends on who you are asking. My idea of success deals mainly with family and life in general. Other's idea of success is dependent on a career, and that's it. So, let's look at the real definition and see what it says. The true definition is "the favorable or prosperous termination of attempts or endeavors, the accomplishment of one's goals; the attainment of wealth, position, honors, or the like." There we have it. Keeping this definition in mind, those who view success as a family and life thing, like myself, and those who view it as a career thing, are both correct. It all depends on your priorities and values.

Now, for argument's sake, we are going to assume that your success is dealing with your career. You are concerned only with work and you want to be as successful with your career as possible. You want to know how best to use time management in obtaining this goal. Okay, let's look at a few ways to do this. Remember, this is focusing on "human-doing" time management only.

First, let me say this. Always, remember to work smart, not hard. Working harder in no way means that you are more productive. You can work your caboose off and get nothing done. This happens all the time. Those who are in this category can easily become entrapped in this cycle of hard non-productive slavery. So, work smart, and this includes good time management choices. Also, keep this in mind: time is the one thing that is the same for everyone and, no matter how much money you have, you can't buy more. It's the same length for everyone and has the same beginning and ending for all of us. Those who are successful never forget these two points. They work smart and stay mindful of time being nonrefundable.

Dale Beaumont, the founder of Business Blueprint, has a few seminars on time management available online. In one of his videos, he talks about time management and gives an example. When I heard him speak, it reminded me of my time-saving method of brushing teeth while doing other things, but he was related to business. He said to use the time driving in the car as a time for planning. He also mentioned Parkinson's law, defined as the notion that work expands to fill the time available for its completion. If there is anyone needing further explaining of this, it's suggesting that your tasks at work will find a way to last as long as you allow them to. This has both positive and negative points and is dependent on how you choose to use it.

The first suggestion of using time management in building a successful career is to always plan your day and never begin that day until the planning is done. Preferably, the planning should be the day or night before—possibly while spending time with the Mrs., but that needs to be incognito. Plan your day in advance. Plan your week in advance. Plan your year in advance. The more planning, the better. Now, let's assume that your day has been planned. It's time now to go to work. Let's go and see what we can do to improve our successes.

Ideally, your career choice itself was based in part on your skills and abilities. Normally, people don't choose a job that is the most difficult for them, and if they do choose that, usually it doesn't last long. So, you have an awareness of what you are good at and what you may not be so good at. That doesn't stop at the very beginning of your career but needs to be factored into all of your decisions which have relevance. Here again, another work smart example. What should you do here? It's simple. Whenever possible, delegate out work that is more difficult or time consuming for you to someone else who can get it done faster and more easily. Here, you need to weigh out the cost/benefit scale. Make sure that the extra costs are warranted and prove to be more beneficial to the overall picture or task.

Another tip for success related to working smart is looking into hiring an expert in certain areas who can either assist you when needed or teach you how to improve in that given area. If paying for an instructor will make you more efficient in the long run, that extra cost is probably worth it, and it helps you with another part of time management. You spend less time on one thing allowing that time to be given to another. One example of what I'm talking about is an accountant hiring a tax preparer for the months of February thru April for doing simple tax returns for those customers allowing the accountant time to work on the more difficult cases. This not only saves the accountant's time but also money because tax preparers can be paid less than accountants, which means that overhead for each billable hour is less. Productivity is increased while the cost is decreased. This is a win-win scenario for any business that I'm aware of.

Delegation of duties, giving responsibilities and duties to someone else, along with permanent and temporary sub-contracting, can be crucial to the success and improvement of any business. This is more than just time management; this is common sense. If it isn't common sense, it certainly should be. If you were to view the itinerary of many successful CEOs, I'm sure that you would be surprised at the actual number of specific duties he or she has. Successful people are marked by their ability to delegate and do it appropriately and in the most beneficial manner possible.

Another tip for success is to use what are known as forced deadlines. Let me add here that this is one area where it's easy to mess things up. We will get to that later, but I'm talking about one of the ugliest curse words known in business: procrastination. It's so easy to put something off if you aren't careful and you are not business savvy. The best way to combat procrastination is by using deadlines because they keep our brains in a state of urgency. It allows us to think of finish lines where we need to be at the front of the race, and those lines not only being at the very end of the task or the day but scattered throughout.

Deadlines will lead you to do or view things a little more efficiently. You will waste less time, will move forward more easily and efficiently, and will have your confidence strengthened. You can also challenge yourself to perform at a better level. What's the difference between a forced deadline and a regular deadline? I have no idea. You can find that in another book. Of course, it's just a joke and wanted to make sure that you are still paying attention. Truthfully, it's like the difference between a big apple and a really big apple. With a forced deadline, the ending or deadline is set with the purpose of speeding up or increasing the efficiency of that particular task. You intend on changing the current trajectory of the task and make it faster or better.

Okay. We've looked at using non-productive time, outsourcing, delegating tasks, sub-contracting, training, application of deadlines, and other tips for successful time management. Now, let's examine a few other ideas and suggestions given by those who have been there and have proven their ideas successful. I want to remind you again that the first step and the absolute most important part of time management is what you want to accomplish with your time and the remembrance that time is irreplaceable and nonrefundable. It can be used only once so do what you think is best for you during that time. This is one area in life where you need to be selfish and choose based on what you want and not what others may want from you. At the end of your life, it is you who will regret it if you don't do this.

At this point in the chapter, I'm going to use another experience of mine as an example of time management. Earlier, I told about my priorities lie with my family over work and how that belief led me to leave a general manager position of a retail and rent-to-own chain. Here is another example from my history with the same company and in the same position where I learned a few things while I was there. Smart and time-savvy businessmen know the importance of staffing; they hire those who are able and will do all duties required of them and those things delegated to them regardless of whether or not those tasks are common or within the scope of their position's job description. If you are instructed by management to do a task, you need to do it or consider finding another job. Management needs to know that once given tasks or additional responsibilities, you will do your job with its additions and will do so correctly, efficiently, and completely. They want you to do this without having to be led the entire way and without the need to be monitored. If you can't be counted on by management, you probably have a short future with that company.

The store where I was employed as a franchise. However, corporate had a clear and precise staffing model and had a guideline based on the number of customers that particular store had. The more customers the store had, the more staffing. I, as the general manager, had the ability to hire as well as terminate any employee at will. So, if I didn't think that an employee was up to standards, I needed to deal with it. I could not blame anyone else for an employee that was bad for business other than me because I had the ability to correct that issue. The problem with that was it was a cumbersome process when it came to hiring and training someone, and it often seemed like it was easier to just forgive an employee for being terrible in efficiency and productivity.

Now, my employer consisted of several different stores. My franchise had around 40 different stores. Anything that happened in my store fell on me, and I was responsible. I got rewarded whenever the store performed well. If there was a problem in my store or a downward slope in business, I had to answer for that. As a matter of fact, that was what determined the length of my employment. There was a weekly comparison of all stores in all areas. If your store remained at the top of the list, you could rest assured that your job was safe for the time being. My store remained at the top, and I intended on it staying that way. Even though my first priority was and is always my family, I gave all that I could to perform well at work. This all came to a point a few months into my career there.

I believed that it was more trouble to hire someone new than it was to just overlook issues with certain employees. I knew that, whether good or bad, I was responsible and had to answer for everything dealing with my store. Not only that, but my income was directly related to the profitability of the store. So, I had no choice but to make sure my store was as efficient and profitable as possible and, at the day's end, the bottom line was all my management would see. All the other details I preferred to keep in the house. This included staffing and each employee's productivity.

I had one employee who was rather intelligent, but he utilized that intelligence in ways that were not the best. First, he knew that whether he did a lot of work or the very minimal work needed to keep his job, his pay will still be the same. He knew that I didn't usually terminate employees because of the difficulty of hiring and training someone new. Lastly, he knew that I did not have the time to watch him make sure that he was actually working. The result of these things was that he did not work much at all–literally and is not blown out of proportion. He was really a terrible employee, but I did the worst thing that I could have and blew my time management away. I started to do his job, along with my own, for him. This was a terrible mistake, and I quickly got locked into the cycle of working hard and producing little. Eventually, he was terminated and someone else was brought on to take his place. Things got much better at that point, and I vowed to never allow myself to get to that point again. The thought that I am trying to point out here is that do not put things off or choose not to do them because of the difficulty. If it is more efficient for the business, then it is best to do it. Most every managerial decision like this one is dealing, in some part, with time management.

We can find many areas in time management to discuss and many examples that can be used, however, I don't want to waste your time, nor do I want to waste my own time rambling. This chapter is about doing things with time management that can better your business and productivity. I believe that we have sufficiently covered this. Here is a recap of what we have discussed.

First, the most important things to remember are those things you see as your priorities. Make your time management coincide with your beliefs and priorities. Once done, you can move on to the next step. Begin to plan your day in advance and never begin your day until after its planning is done. Look at the areas of your non-productive time and see where you can add things, such as planning, to better utilize that time. When planning work activities, choose to delegate or contract out when it is best. You can also outsource whenever it will increase productivity and save you time. Choose staff wisely and never put off doing something because it may be a difficult or time-consuming task. Better to get it done and over with. Set goals and prioritize. Allow yourself to learn from others who may be better or smarter in certain areas. Reread this chapter and this book as many times as necessary for you to remember most of what you learn while reading it.

The final point that will be noted in this chapter is the common link between successful people and their personalities. As with every other part of a successful business, there needs to be an element of assertiveness. Assertive people tend to be more successful in business, among other things. They are diligent and strong in their convictions. They can commonly say no; they are not easily swayed or distracted from their chosen path. Those who are more assertive are more likely to become leaders rather than followers. This is just as true with time management as it is with the other parts of the business. In planning, you need to set clear and concise goals, be unwavering in what it is that you seek, and be willing to work for it. These characteristics are the key to success and successful planning. Assertiveness can be learned or acquired. So, if you aren't assertive now, work on becoming that way. It will prove extremely beneficial with time management.

Chapter 12: To Do List Apps

Technology has changed the way we do so many things, and that includes how we manage your time. You could argue that technology has zapped our time supplies, because we spend so much time checking our Facebook pages, reading Twitter, and perusing Instagram, to no real productive end. We also spend far too much time checking our emails, when less often would be perfectly fine too!

Technology has streamlined many things to our advantage, and there are many to do list and time management apps on the market, which can help with productivity. Not everyone prefers to do things electronically, but it is something to consider. Let's compare the two.

The Old-Fashioned Way or Let Technology Help?

If you're not sure which way to go, let's compare the two methods and see which has the most pros and cons in either direction.

Using a Time Management App

Apps on the market either can be literal to do list template that you simply run yourself, or they can have lots of different features to make use of, such as alarms and reminders, notes and adjustment guides. There are free versions and there are ones that you pay for; it depends how much use you get out of the app as to whether you would consider paying for it or not.

Pros of Using an App

- You can use your app anywhere, so if you're sat on the bus or walking down the street, you can see what your progress is like for that day or week

- You can add items to your list very quickly and easily

- Your app may have many other features, such as reminders and tools which help you stay on track

- There are a wide variety of choices on the market, both free and paid, so you can find the best app for you by shopping around and comparing

- Readjusting your to do list when a new task comes in is much easier and less messy when using an app

Cons of Using an App

- If your phone is lost or stolen, or even if it breaks, you are left without your app and therefore your list

- You are at the mercy of your phone battery!

- Some people prefer the feel of crossing off or ticking off an item literally on a piece of a paper

- Some apps can be quite complicated to figure out at first and may have more features than you need

Using a Traditional Method

By 'traditional method' we are talking about a piece of paper/specific notebook and a pen or pencil. You would write a list and cross things off as you go, or you could draw up your table and personalize it to your needs.

Pros of Using a Traditional Method

- You can see very clearly in front of you what you need to do

- Many people prefer the feel of crossing off items physically, as it gives a real sense of accomplishment and a buzz

- You can cross things out easily

- It is a much more simple format, which is easy for everyone to use

Cons of Using a Traditional Method

- You could easily lose your list, and then you would be left floundering!

- If you have to adjust and move things around, your list could end up very messy and hard to understand/read

- You are missing out on the extra features that come with an app

- Finding a specific format could be difficult when simply writing out a list, e.g. columns

How to Use a Pen and Paper Format

To give you a real overview of the right type of to-do list for you, we are now going to quickly talk about how to use a paper format of a to-do list. You might think that it's undoubtedly a no-brainer, but to get the most out of this particular type of list, you need to think of a few different options.

If you're not going to make use of technology here, you're best to purchase yourself a notebook in which you write your lists. If you have a single piece of paper or a post-it notes hanging around, you're much more likely to lose it, which would be a minor disaster. You're much more likely to stick to your list and use it if you have a useful and pleasant place you write it all down. Also, look for a notebook that has a loop for a pen or pencil, and then you're never going to be frantically searching around for a lost pen!

For a simple home to do list, a small flip notebook would be sufficient, and you can easily slip into a pocket or your bag. For a work list, it is better to go for an A5 version, with a hardback option easier to write in. You might be wondering why you need to think about the specifics of your notebook, but if you want to make the best of the situation, and make it easier for you, these small details will make a huge difference.

For a simple home to do list, you just need a page a day, and you will write down all the jobs you need to do that day, ticking them off as you go along. The priority side of it isn't as important here, but to make the most of your time, sit down in the morning when you write the list, and number the tasks from 1 to whatever, in the order you're going to do them – 1 being the most important.

For the A5 type of to-do list, you can either draw columns in your book or simply write it all down in list format. Have a page per week, perhaps turning the page to landscape view, and remember to date when you add tasks to the list. This will help you see how old tasks are. You should write the task, how important it is, and then cross it off as you go.

Using a traditional method is certainly the easiest way, but it does lack all singing, all dancing, and beneficial features of an app.

Best to Do List Apps

Now we have talked about a traditional method versus a technological method; we need to give you some insight into the best time management apps currently on the market. The range is huge, but we have picked out some of the best, regarding ease of use, features, and overall production capacity.

Google Keep

This is certainly one of the best to do list apps around, and the good news is that it's free on Android and iOS! The design is simple and easy to use, and while it does have added features, such as allowing you to add voice and written notes, pictures and put your tasks into categories, these are very simple to incorporate and won't give you a headache while you're trying to work yours around the app! You are also able to invite other people to add tasks to your to-do list (useful for work collaborations). You don't only have to make a to-do list here; you can add a shopping list to work alongside your main list too!

The only typical downside of this particular app is that many users didn't like the alarm and reminder system, but the simplicity of the rest of it makes it a great choice for first-time users.

Todoist

This is one of the most comprehensive to-do list apps you will find on the market, and because of that, you will need to pay for it. This isn't going to break the bank, however, as you the premium version will cost you around $30 per year currently. The free version will give you enough to do simple planning tasks, and that may be enough for you overall.

This particular app allows you to pair it up with your social media accounts, for easy signing in, and setting it all up is very easy indeed. You can add in tasks at any time, and you can assign priorities and deadlines, to highlight the most important ones quickly and clearly. Regarding ticking off your tasks, you simply click a box, and you'll feel a sense of pride as you do so!

The premium features, the ones you pay for, include reminders, extra comments, and having a backup system, so you don't lose anything important.

Evernote

Evernote has long been a popular option for note taking, but you can also utilize it's time management options to create an excellent to do list. The app allows you to take notes, add reminders, add voice memos, and even photos, and you can add extra documents if you need to, such as those from Word or PDFs. When you add anything to your list, it will sync across all devices, so you don't have to worry about having to update everything more than once, if you have the app installed on your tablet and your phone, for example.

The free version is more than enough for a regular user, but you can upgrade to the premium account for a small fee, which is around $35 or $70 per year currently, depending on which package you opt for. There are countless extras with the paid versions, such as being able to add to your list when you're offline, extra storage, and a password protection feature.

Wunderlist

Wunderlist has long been used as a free version for those who don't want anything too smart and fancy, and who just want a simple and easy to use app that exactly does what it is supposed to do. That sums Wunderlist up perfectly.

Again, you can opt for the free version, or you can upgrade to the premium version, for around $60 per year currently, but there are plenty of features on the free version, so it's worth trying that one first and see how you get along. This particular version allows you to create lists and invite collaborators (up to 25 at one time), as well as being able to add reminders and notes to your lists. The premium version gives you extras, such as being able to add notes and documents. For those who simply want to organize their work or home tasks, the free version of Wunderlist is very hard to beat.

Microsoft To Do

If you regularly work with Microsoft Office, this particular app (free) is ideal for syncing everything together. Because of the brand name, you can expect quality, and that's really what you get. The app was first created by Wanderlist and was then bought by Microsoft, so it utilizes the best of both worlds. The simple way in which the app works is very similar to the Wanderlist version too, and that is a definite plus.

You can easily set up tasks and add in memos and reminders, but there is another built-in feature, called My Day. This means you can create a daily list which runs alongside your main task list, and from there you can organize both together. You are taking tasks from your main weekly or monthly list and allotting them to a day, and from there you're prioritizing them in order. It is much easier in practice than it sounds in words!

Clear To-dos

Again, if you want something which is very easy to use and which doesn't add extra clutter to your day, Clear To-dos is a good option. The downside is that this particular app isn't currently available on Android, and you can only download it for iOS.

The layout of this particular app may be simple, but it looks classy at the same time. You can customize its appearance, e.g., background color and font, etc., so you can make it even easier to understand, while also looking the part at the same time! You can also sync everything between your Apple devices through the app and iCloud, so you're never missing important information from one device to the next.

The app is free to a point, but after a certain amount of usage, you will hit what is referred to as a 'paywall.' If you prefer to pay once and be done with it, then another app may be better, but for moderate usage on a daily basis, this is a good go for choice.

These are six of the best and most popular to do list and time management tools on the market currently. Remember to review and change your app as you see fit constantly – the way you work may not stay static constantly, and you might need to change things around a little, as your work changes, or as demand occurs.

Regarding whether you should go for free versions or pay for a premium option, this is something only you can decide. The best course of action, however, is to go for a free version first and try the app out for size. This will give you a feel of whether it is going to work for you or not, and if it does, and you like it enough to use the extra features, then perhaps try the premium version for a month. If after that month you don't feel it's worth it, you can always cancel your subscription (check the small print) and try a different option.

Finding the best to do list app is partly by trial and error, so be prepared to do a little experimentation on your journey towards task organization and time management!

DISTINGUISH BETWEEN TIMEBOXING AND THE TIME CHUNKING METHOD

Timeboxing and the time chunking method offer different methods for accomplishing similar goals.

TIMEBOXING WAS AROUND LONG before time chunking became popular. It's a method for limiting the amount of time allocated to a particular task or project. At the end of a timebox, the individual evaluates his or her progress on the activity at hand, and asks a simple question: "Does the work I've completed satisfy the job requirements?"

If the answer is yes, no more work is performed on the task or project. If the answer is no, further time boxes are scheduled as needed.

Timeboxing was originally created as a way for teams to manage projects. The goal was to reduce the likelihood that a given project would extend past its scope. In doing so, timeboxing helps the individual or team to meet the project's deadline.

One of the benefits of using time boxes in this manner is that it prevents you from falling prey to Parkinson's Law. That law states that "work expands so as to fill the time available for its completion." If you allot 4 hours for a particular activity, that activity is likely to require 4 hours to complete. If you allot 1 hour, you're likely to complete it in 1 hour.

With timeboxing, you establish a limited time frame during which you'll work on an activity. Committing to that time frame sets a deadline. It forces you to work toward the completion of the activity rather than simply spending time working on it. Importantly, it also discourages perfectionism.

Chapter 13: Timeboxing Vs. Time Chunking Method

The time chunking method is a type of timeboxing strategy. As we discussed at the beginning of this guide, it encourages you to work for 25-minute segments and take 5-minute breaks between them. (Again, I strongly recommend testing different durations and creating a modified time chunking system that complements your natural workflow and ability to focus.)

The duration of a time box can technically vary from a few minutes to several months. It depends on the activity or project. The latter might involve hundreds of individual tasks.

The time chunking method is intended to keep you on task. As we covered in Step 2, it was created with the idea that the brain can only focus for short periods of time. After that time elapses, it needs a short break.

Timeboxing was designed to manage projects in such a way that time isn't wasted on them. Again, it discourages perfectionism.

With the time chunking method, you have the flexibility to cater to your perfectionist tendencies. You can devote as many time chunks as you desire to a task. There's no formal evaluation step that forces you to assess your progress and determine if you've met a project's requirements.

That's a huge difference from timeboxing. With timeboxing, you set a deadline - for example, 2 hours - for each activity. The deadline is flexible. If, when it arrives, you haven't met the activity's requirements, you estimate the amount of additional time you need to devote to it and create another time box. Even though the deadline is flexible, it pushes you toward completion. It quiets your inner perfectionist and helps you focus on "shipping."

It's a powerful tool for increasing your productivity. So that begs the question...

Which Should You Choose: Timeboxing Or The Time Chunking Method?

In a word, both.

Your productivity is influenced by two things:

1. your ability to focus on the task at hand

2. your ability to ship

The time chunking method addresses your ability to focus, but not your ability to ship (at least, not directly). Timeboxing addresses your ability to ship, but not your ability to focus (at least, not directly).

Why not use both techniques simultaneously to address both issues? Here's an example:

Suppose you're writing a long blog post. From your experience writing similar blogs in the past, you know you can complete the first draft in 2 hours. Start with timeboxing. Set aside 2 hours to complete the draft. Now, use the time chunking method to break that 2-hour chunk into several work segments.

If you're using a typical time chunking model, your schedule will look like the following:

- Work for 25 minutes

- Take a 5-minute break

- Work for 25 minutes

- Take a 5-minute break

- Work for 25 minutes

- Take a 5-minute break

- Work for 25 minutes

- Take a 15-minute break

- Work for 20 minutes to complete the task

That equals 2 hours of work.

Personally, I'd used a modified model that caters to my own natural workflow. It would look like the following:

- Work for 50 minutes

- Take a 10-minute break

- Work for 50 minutes

- Take a 10-minute break

- Work for 20 minutes

- Take a 20-minute break

The point is that the time chunking method can work seamlessly with timeboxing to increase your daily output. Each is flexible enough to accommodate the other.

Some people swear by timeboxing and claim they wouldn't be able to work in any other fashion. Others swear by the time chunking method and make similar claims about its effectiveness. But there's no reason to choose between them. Use them both.

This guide is obviously about using the time chunking method. For that reason, I'm not devoting a significant amount of time on other time management strategies. But it's worth mentioning timeboxing as an important complement to using time chunks.

I encourage you to try it. In addition to working within time chunks, set time boxes that limit the amount of time you spend on projects. You'll find that it will cure you of your perfectionism. That alone will be a major step toward boosting your productivity.

Chapter 14: What to Do When You Start Feeling Overwhelmed

The first thing that you need to appreciate is that everyone feels overwhelmed at some time in their career and home life. Organization helps you to feel this less, but you may still get times when you really don't know how you are going to manage everything that you have to do. There are important points that you need to remember which you may not see as work related, although they will relate to your performance in work and at home. Make sure that you follow the advice given below because it's vital. Here are some tactics that you can use to make yourself feel less overwhelmed:

- Get a decent night's sleep every night
- Try to switch off from work once you have lined up your work for tomorrow
- Switch off your cell phone after hours
- Learn to delegate
- Make sure you are having adequate breaks

The tendency of people who are overwhelmed is to over-do it even more because they are worried about keeping up with work and home commitments. However, if you follow the four pieces of advice given above, you are putting yourself in good stead and the rest is easy. Let's go into some of things that you may find difficult:

Your workload is too heavy – If you have too much work, and you are a little bit of a perfectionist, chances are that you do too much of the work yourself. Learn to delegate and involve other people, both on the work and home front because when you learn to trust others, you can share that workload and still achieve the same amount. The way to do this with work is to assign part of the load to people you believe capable of doing that work and making sure that you include a diary reminder so that you can check that it's being done. Look on your to-do list and work out how much of it you can delegate so that your list is more manageable. Then, make sure that each task on the list is adequately broken into small parts. Often you can delegate parts of the job to others and then do a report on the whole job when everyone has done their part of it. The weight doesn't have to fall completely on your shoulders and if you split the job into manageable parts, you actually take better control of it because it's easier to complete small tasks than trying to fulfill a whole huge task on your own.

At home, be honest with your partner about the amount of work that you have and enlist your partner's help in doing the mundane time consuming things that are getting you down. In a partnership, you really can take on more together and if you are honest about feeling overwhelmed, your partner will be glad to step in occasionally to help you with all of those commitments.

Assess your job - Everyone needs to do this from time to time and if you know better ways that more can be done, don't be afraid to have a meeting with your boss to discuss this. There may be some company policies that are getting you down. There may, for instance, be too many meetings eating into your productive time. If your boss can scale these down to only the necessary ones, that will give you more time to do all the things on your to-do list in a timely fashion. If you find that you are being laden with more work than you originally did, it's actually a compliment because it shows that your boss trusts you, but you do need to tell him/her if you need more team members or more expertise in fields that are taking up too much of your time.

Assess your workload - At times when you are overwhelmed sit back and examine all the things on the to-do list. Don't worry about them. Simply work out the priorities as some will have less priority than others. The problem is that people who do get overwhelmed tend to see the whole list and panic. Breathe deeply and look realistically at the list and change the priorities, getting those jobs out the way that you can, so as to make your list more manageable. Look for jobs that you can delegate easily and move these. They can be dealt with, with the same level of urgency, but they don't necessarily need to be dealt with by you. Look at things that can wait until tomorrow and take these off the to-do list for today, as the sheer fact that the list is too long is what is worrying you. Make sure you mark them onto tomorrow's list.

What you need to be sure of is that you are not being overwhelmed by overthinking things. Often people spend more time worrying than actually being productive. If you can examine your list, decide upon your priorities and delegate where possible, your list will become smaller and more manageable. Then you will be able to attack it with more confidence that you can finish it. If you have never tried it, take a break and do not take your phone with you. Think of nothing that is remotely associated with work and remember that a break should be just that – a break away from everything. The reason this becomes so important is that you manage to go back to your work with a fresh outlook and less procrastination. That little break, whether for a coffee or for lunch, helps your mind to rest so that when you do go back to the tasks at hand, you do so with a mind that is capable of taking on the workload with less worry. Worry leads to procrastination and procrastination leads to under-achievement. Thus, avoid it. Take a break and go back into your work full swing.

The difference to being busy or feeling busy

We tend to believe we are busy based on how much we do. The more things we have to finish, the busier we are. And the less tasks we have, the laxer and "lazier" we are. And yet we can feel busy even when we don't have much stuff to do, or relaxed in the midst of chaos. The states of "busy" and "not busy" aren't easily defined by what we do or what we don't. Again, the brain can only do so little things at once. Being busy is more of a state of mind, anyway.

What's the Priority when I'm feeling Overwhelmed?

Humans are the only creatures in nature that resist status quo. We want to have fun in the sun or go to cities that never sleep. Yet natural ebbs such as darkness between days and the time between seasons are natural and necessary. The message is clear: if you are feeling tired, then rest. Rest like the rest of nature does in times of change.

What If I Don't Have Enough Time?

There are only so many hours our bodies can function for before they start to feel fatigue. With fatigue, you make more mistakes, feel exhausted, more prone to fighting, and find you aren't thinking as well off as you should. That's the first problem with time. The second is that time is finite, constantly dwindling away by the second. Many of us don't have much time left to invest, and in trying to make up more time, we sacrifice sleep.

Yet sleep is very important. Sleeping for less than even an hour needed greatly reduces our cognitive capacities. So in trying to make up more time with less sleep, you cut away from the quality of your work otherwise, causing more harm than good to yourself. So don't try to manage time better. Manage your energy.

Do I have to do everything myself?

You shouldn't. Doing all the work yourself increases the burden on yourself and prevents others from doing their part. Everyone should get a chance to shine. Delegate yourself more to home and work, while using your free time for the things you love to do.

What would it take for me to say No?

Most people may claim to give in to sudden requests because they do not want to let their fellow co-workers down. However, this could be more about not wanting to let themselves down, and to feel needed. If we take a look at ourselves, we would want others to come to us so we can help them, even for the little things.

We handle disruption immediately because if we don't do so now, then when? It's important to be reasonably accessible to the people you live and work with, but you shouldn't spend most of your waking hours helping them when you have your own tasks to finish. It's better to prioritize your own needs, recognize your own limits, and not needlessly multitask. That's when to say "no".

Bob Carter once said "Poor planning on your part does not necessitate and emergency on mine". At times you will feel the need to help out a sudden request by a coworker, but you need to recognize when it is necessary to drop what you are doing to help, and learn to say "no" so you can manage your own work efficiently.

Is My Stuff Taking Over My Life?

Many people seem to suffer from a similar problem with clutter: tons of papers and magazines, overflowing garages with unopened boxes, closets stuffed like clothing department retailer stores, and so on. This is a real problem as the inability to be organized and feeling that "the stuff" takes over our sense of selves. The need to own so many things leads to certain consequences. Kids are overstimulated by the collection, and they lose the ability to focus or concentrate. Finances pile up because of misplaced bills and over-purchasing. Neither party of the couple lets up wanting to sell or let go of their possessions. This also goes on.

Taking control of the house is an important first step; there is danger in the outside world, stability in home can ensure safety and some semblance of peace. The clutter might be overwhelming and stressful, but if one removes the problem of the clutter, then everything will be better.

Is Stress Bad?

When you get stressed, your body produces protective chemicals and increase activity in your immune cells to boost defense. Your body and brain get a boost from this. This burst of stress, believe it or not, can starve off disease, make vaccinations stronger, and even protect against certain types of cancer. Small amounts of stress also boost your memory. However, too much stress is definitely a bad thing. That's why there needs to be a balance. Too less stress does nothing to trigger your body's defenses and can leave you bored. But too much and you'll become cranky, tired and sick.

What happens when I feel Anxiety?

Sometimes it's better to accept when you're feeling anxiety and focus what is in front of you. Trying to squelch or deny it will only make the feeling worse. If you're at interview, a party, or another sort of social event, make contact and listen to them. Be conscious of what you're saying when you get the chance to speak. So when you're feeling anxiety, try to face the problem head on. Just be sure to take deep breaths every so often to allow the anxious thoughts to drift away.

How Do I Stop Focusing on the Clock?

It is akin to spiritual practice to remove yourself from time, as removing your awareness of time means striking away your own ego.

The first step in doing so is to step out of the "time dimension" as often as possible. Learn to live in the moment. Make it your practice to withdraw attention from what happened before or what will happen later as they're not relevant to the time now.

Step two is to be present as the watcher of your mind. Be aware of your thoughts, emotions, and reactions in various situations. Be at least as interested in your reactions towards certain situations or people.

The third and final step is to use your senses fully. Look around, but don't interpret what you see. Be aware of the space that allows everything. Listen to the sounds, and the silence. Touch anything and feel its very Being.

This zen-ness state may not make much sense, but the more you distance and distract yourself from the clock and time, the more you can just cut back and let loose.

Chapter 15: The Importance of Taking Breaks

Right now, ask yourself how many breaks you take each day, and how long each of those breaks is (on average). Are you the kind of person who will set aside large amounts of times meant for getting work done and then try and get as much work done within that time, or are you the kind of person who will work, take a short break, work a little more, take another short break, work a little more, another short break, and so on?

Taking breaks are important for becoming more productive and appropriately managing your time. Granted, you obviously can't take too many breaks to the point that it lowers the amount of time that you have for actually getting things done, but you should take several breaks a day.

If you ever feel mentally and physically drained at the end of each day, then it's a clear indication that you're not taking enough breaks. And when you begin feeling mentally and physically drained in the first place, it's ultimately more difficult to get work done.

Just regular 5-10 minute breaks can give you enough physical rest and mental relaxation time to get yourself back in the swing of things. As a general rule of thumb, we recommend that you make it a habit to take at least one 5-10 minute break for every hour of work.

Ultimately, that's going to add up to roughly an hour (or perhaps a little more) of time in your day that you could have spent working. Why not spend that hour getting more things done? Well, there are multiple reasons for why you should take that 10-minute break for every hour of work. Here are the most important ones:

Breaks Make Your Productivity Increase

Multiple studies have virtually confirmed that those who take a short break an hour will have a better work performance than those who do not. The reason why is because if you work continuously nonstop, other than for maybe a brief lunch break, your mind can become numb. As a result, the job you are doing becomes less and less important to you. Your energy becomes drained, and you may begin to work at your task like a robot rather than an actual person.

Take a break to allow you to clear your mind and come back to the task with new energy. That's why those who set aside 5-10 minutes of break time for every hour of work will not only achieve more work on any given day, but their actual work will be of a higher quality as well.

Breaks Make You More Creative

Taking a short break every hour won't just make you more productive, it also makes you more creative! Remember how we just said that working continuously can make your mind become numb? If you keep at it that way, you will be significantly less likely of gaining a new insight into things. But if you take a break and allow your mind to refresh, you'll be able to re-approach the task with a new perspective. Think of a 5-10 minute break as being a recharge for your brain to re-increase your levels of creativity.

Breaks Are Good For Your Physical Health

As humans, our bodies are not physically designed to just sit down at a desk all day. We need to get up and move around. It ensures that our blood continues circulating properly and that our brain receives more oxygen. Even simply getting up and walking around the office for 5 minutes after every hour of work is good for your health physically speaking.

Breaks Offer You A Chance To Do Something Stimulating

When we say take a break, we don't just mean that you stand up and stretch and grab a new cup of coffee. We mean that you need to do something stimulating. Something short, but something that challenges your mind.

Now absolutely, you need to stand up from your chair and move around. That much is certain. But you should still do more than just grabbing that new cup of coffee and checking your e-mail. Maybe instead, play a fun but short app on your phone that causes your mind to think or for you to make quick reactions. Or maybe you can use that time to brainstorm ideas for another project you have going on as a hobby.

Breaks Offer You A Change Of Scenery

Finally, your desk and computer are never exactly the most inspiring scenery, right? Always use your break as an opportunity to get out of your office space and to get a new change of scenery; the change of scenery will always be better for you if it's outside rather than the stagnant inside office. Being outside for just five minutes will be relaxing for both your mind and body and enough to recharge or motivate you for the next hour of work.

Chapter 16: How To Make Your To-Do List Sustainable

I understand you perfectly—it is extremely frustrating not to finish or move forward with your To-Do List. Many times, although your surroundings are optimal for work or study, it is your thoughts that sabotage your best attempts to concentrate. Trying to dodge the many distractions, excuses, etc., seems an impossible mission that only ninjas with great mastery of mind can achieve.

However, the good thing is that this chapter is the right path for you. In this chapter, I'll explain how to train your mind to concentrate better in order to stick to the right path while creating the correct To-Do List.

Before that, it is essential for you to recognize that in order to keep this To-Do List sustainable, you must stay focus and not be distracted. Let me bring you through the 2 main types of distraction and how to stay focused instead.

Types of distractions

There are two classifications for all those distractions:

1. External distractions: unexpected visits, phone calls, spontaneous commitments, emails, mobile notifications, messages, etc.

2. Internal distractions: thoughts, desires, impulses, worries, and ideas.

You may notice that the internal are relatively few, but these are the most problematic for a simple reason: because you create them yourself. They are the product of your cognition, your thoughts and your memories.

All start with a thought that appears in your mind. For example: "How many?" "I like this." "What about my pictures on Facebook, Twitter, and Instagram?" The impulse is so great that you can't resist following the course of this thought, which distracts you. It is only when you manage to control your own mind that you can easily avoid these kinds of thoughts.

But the question that many people ask is: Why can't we control these thoughts? Why do we lose control of the rudder and lose our attention? The answer is simple. It's because in your daily life, you train your brain to be distracted without realizing.

ADD (Attention Deficit Disorder) is a psychological condition whereby people are unable to concentrate on something for extended periods of time. Although this condition is fairly common, not everyone suffers it.

Ed Hallowell, a former professor at Harvard Medical School, says that we have generated a "cultural attention deficit."

We have trained our brains to change attention over and over again, losing the ability to focus on one thing.

Bouncing between one activity and another seems like merely a bad habit; however, it is even more than that. These abrupt changes of attention between activities weaken your mental strength to keep your attention on one thing. You become addicted to variety and compulsively wish to direct your attention to something new, such as a spontaneous thought, a notification, or a new activity.

The problem is that when we really want to concentrate, it is impossible. Your mind laughs out loud, thinking it's a joke. Satisfying the deep desire to distract yourself is like spoiling your mind to instant gratification.

While it sounds strange, it is normal to fight against your deepest desires all the time. According to a study, the three main desires against which we fight all day are: sex, sleep and eating. But the list also includes the desire to distract you with a rewarding, easy and novel activity.

How do you train your mind to concentrate on just two steps when creating your To-Do List?

It seems like an easy question to answer. But be careful, as there are thousands of tips trying to address that question that don't really work. Everything depends on the type of activity. So, then, I'm going to explain three main rules before seeing what techniques you can use to increase your concentration.

The three main rules before applying the techniques

Rule #1: Your activity doesn't have to be a usual distraction

Many activities are discarded because they don't train your attention but weaken it. For example, if you constantly have the impulse to check your mail, change the television channel or review the news on Facebook or Instagram, then they are discarded activities.

Rule #2: Your activity has to be individual

It is about improving your connection with your thoughts and managing to control them while maintaining your attention.

However, when someone else catches your attention, the exercise is no longer effective.

Rule #3: Your activity can't be unhealthy

If the activity trains your attention but harms your health, the purpose of improving your life doesn't make sense. For example: eating unhealthy foods or smoking are activities that are discarded.

Now, if you accept the rules, you can continue reading to see the two main techniques to increase your concentration when creating your To-Do List.

Techniques to stay focused when creating your To-Do List

Technique #1: Choose a daily activity

Evaluate your daily routine and choose a simple activity (with a short duration) to which you can direct your attention fully for a few minutes (and that complies with the three rules you just read). That is, it is about being aware of what you are doing, directing all your attention and all your senses towards that activity for a short period of time.

These are some examples:

- Brush your teeth

- Wash the dishes

- Read a book

- Listen to music

- Make your bed

- Floss

- Draw or color

- Have a coffee or tea

- Read the newspaper

- Eat an apple

This type of activity can be done in a mindfulness way to help you to feel better, to enjoy the moment, and above all to train your mind to focus on only one thing at a time, controlling the impulse of distraction.

In this way, instead of training your mind to distract, you are doing the opposite: you are training your mind to concentrate. This long and short-term training helps you to have control of your thoughts when you really need to do it.

Technique #2: Identify your invading thoughts

Earlier on, I mentioned "types of distractions", where our thoughts are a type of internal distractions. You may wonder: what should I do during that activity to focus my attention? What do I do if thoughts or impulses suddenly arise?

If you detect any thought, concern, desire or impulse, simply identify that it is there, be aware of it and let it go. Gently return your attention to your activity.

For example, if you choose to wash your hair or brush your teeth and concentrate on that activity, but suddenly you start thinking about the numerous clothes that you need to wash for the day, then it means that your training is not working. You have to do be aware that thought appeared, then gently refocus on the movement of the brush or the cool water.

Little by little, you will learn to tame your mind. It's about not getting carried away by all the thoughts in your head, not trying to eliminate them.

Strategies

- When you have a task to complete, divide it into smaller and digestible tasks.

- Then take one of those sub-tasks, and write in a list form the sequence of steps you have to follow to complete it successfully.

- Mark as done according to the progress of each step.

- Don't write a list a mile long that you can never complete, or plan your day in such a way that you will be running from one place to another.

- Leave some space for breaks.

You are free to deviate from the course if necessary, but the structure of a general plan will help you keep your journey on the right track.

You will see how easy it is to avoid getting distracted because your mind gets hooked on the feeling of achievement and progress, which improves your productivity enormously.

In addition, this strategy gives you a feeling of "flow" or constant progress, which at the same time trains your ability to concentrate better and better.

Chapter 17: Dumping Time-Wasters

There are many issues we carry around that not only rob us of good health and strong bodies, but they are an incredible waste of time. Most of them are bad habits we've picked up over the years. While they might not have been so harmful when we were in our 20s, as we mature our practices take their toll on our time, productivity, and personal well-being.

Smoking

Smoking is probably one of the most time-consuming habits on the planet. Not only do workers take unscheduled breaks to feed the nasty habit of smoking, but the damage smoking does to workers' immune systems, and overall health causes untold time lost in sickness and absenteeism. Smokers have less energy, focus, and productivity, creating a working environment that places additional responsibility on others to pick up the slack and the smokers to work excessive hours to get their job completed.

You figure, most smokers take at least six 10-15-minute breaks a day to go outside for a cigarette. That adds up to over an hour a day spent smoking that could have been used to get more work done. Because smokers take so many breaks during the day, they then find it necessary to stay late to accomplish their goals at night. If they stay an hour later in the evening, that's an hour more out of their personal time with family.

So, if you're a smoker and looking to save time so you can enjoy your family, do yourself an enormous favor. Stop smoking. Not only will you have more time during the day, but you'll live a longer more active life.

Personal Grooming

If you're spending more than 45 minutes to an hour a day in personal grooming, that's time that could go toward having more fun. At the risk of sounding like a sexist, excessive time spent grooming is usually a female issue. If you fall into this category, you might need to consider an easier-to-maintain hairstyle or maybe less elaborate make-up. Experiment a bit to see how you can cut down on your time grooming. It's understandable if you don't want to cut your hair, but figure out how you can braid it or put it up several days a week to save yourself time.

Unhealthy Eating Habits

You wouldn't think that eating healthier could save you time, right? Well, think again! When you regularly eat unhealthy food, it usually includes a lot of the fast food variety. That means you're taking longer lunch breaks, driving to the restaurant, and then carrying it back to work. If you're buying for several co-workers, you're taking their orders, collecting the money, dividing the food, eating, and cleaning the mess. All of this takes time. Wouldn't it be quicker and healthier to bring a salad from home or pack a healthier lunch?

Also, eating unhealthy or over-eating can make you listless after lunch. If you can't take a physical nap, you take a mental one. Your eyes glaze over, you have trouble focusing, and your productivity slows down. Eating healthier provides more energy and keeps you alert and ready to meet the afternoon's challenges. Also, if you continue to overeat or eat unhealthy in the evening, your sleep is often interrupted, and your digestion is disturbed.

Substance Abuse

People who abuse alcohol or drugs are terrible time wasters, and their habits are even worse for your health and productivity than smoking or over-eating. Your whole system is thrown off by repeated substance abuse, and your ability to problem solve is impaired. Your body and mind become stressed to the point where you do not think or act rationally. Your work is not accurate, so much of it requires time-consuming revisions.

Ongoing substance abuse doesn't go unnoticed in the workplace. Your co-workers resent having to fill the gap your poor performance creates and management recognizes the negative impact you bring to the workplace. If it continues, you'll get your walking papers, and the company has now wasted all that time training you. Worse of all, you have regretfully wasted your potential.

A Perfectionists Attitude

A corporation's highest productivity doesn't usually originate with those striving for perfection. If you're picking apart every little detail to make your project perfect, you're not earning your keep. Most companies don't require perfection; they need productivity. If it takes you an hour to balance the cash drawer when it was only a nickel off, wouldn't it have been a better use of your time just to put a nickel in the drawer and call it good? If your desire is to use your time wisely, make sure the cost of the time you take trying to be perfect is worth your while.

Emotional Issues

If you're having personal issues, leave them at the door of your workplace. Likewise, if you have stress at work, talk it over with your significant other but don't bring it into your personal space. Emotional issues can cause you to stretch a five-minute chewing out from the boss into a two-week pout if you take things too personally. There are going to be times when you must take a bit of constructive criticism, so hear what's being discussed, let it roll off your back, make any adjustments or changes that are necessary, and then move forward. Punishing yourself for weeks isn't going to make you or your boss happy about the situation. So, lift yourself up, brush it off, and get back to work determined more than ever to put your best foot forward.

If your personal life is a train wreck, don't share it with everybody at work. First of all, they don't need to know your business. Peers won't feel empathetic toward you; instead, they'll just think you are a mental mess. Besides, the company won't appreciate the time you waste sharing your personal issues with all who will listen, especially when you're doing it on the company's dime.

Unnecessary Communications

Talking on your personal cell phone at work is a huge waste of company time. Don't think your supervisor doesn't know that's what's going on with your lack of productivity. If you want to surf the Internet, find another place to do it than at work. It shouldn't surprise you that most larger companies monitor your Internet use and email posts. Speaking of emails, don't let them rule your day. In fact, it's a good idea not to check your emails first thing every morning. Work your time-management plan, and save the emails for a while until you've accomplished a few things on your "to-do" list.

If you discover its more time efficient to pick up the phone or just walk down the hall for a brief meeting, rather than email back and forth for twenty minutes, then do it. Get out of your chair and have a face-to-face with your co-worker. The same holds true with texting. Avoid spending twenty minutes texting back and forth when a five-minute phone call could have settled things.

Insisting on DIY Projects

Stop trying to do everything yourself; self-sacrifice is not heroic, it's a time waster. If delegated part of the project to someone who is more qualified and who can give it immediate attention saves time, then stop making every project a DIY.

Commuting

Most people have at least a 30-minute commute to work each day. That's an hour of your time that you could use more productively. For example, you could listen to self-help books on tape. Motivational leaders could inspire you, or you could dictate to your assistant some daily tasks you'd like to see accomplished. If you take public transportation to work, you could use your commute time to read or make your "to do" list for the day on your way to work and plan the next day's tasks on your way home.

Television

There are programs on television that are quite entertaining and educational, but for the most part, it is a huge time waster. If you are sitting in front of the television every evening for two to three hours, that's a lot of time you could spend doing something more productive. You could give yourself a creative outlet, or plan your meals for the week. Or, you could take a hike with your children or take the dog for a walk. There is a whole world outside your flat screen. If you're looking for a bigger picture than your 65-inch offers, try the great outdoors.

Worry and Anxiety

So many people who sacrifice today because they spend their time worrying about what happened yesterday or what could happen tomorrow. What a waste of the day! Live in the present. When you think about it, today is all you have, and right now is the only time that you can change. When you are preoccupied with worry, you can't focus, and your accuracy suffers because you've got your mind on other things besides what needs doing today.

You've probably heard people say that worry never changed anything, but I beg to differ. Anxiety makes things so much worse than if you had looked at the issue through a more positive lens. Sometimes the only thing standing between an anxious attitude and a positive one is making the decision to change your perspective.

No Time-Management Plan

The biggest time waster you can have is when you have no time-management plan. It's not that you haven't worked hard all day, but that you haven't worked smart. You've let interruptions and distractions, a failure to set your priorities, and maybe even procrastination to get in the way of any time-saving strategies you could have implemented to make your day productive. You cannot expect to make the best use of your time when you don't know what or how to accomplish things in the most efficient manner possible.

Without a plan, all you've got is hope that you'll be able to complete your work. With no or poor planning, time flies by, and you end up with way too much work at the end of your day.

If you need to complete your job by tomorrow, there's nothing for it but to stay late and finish. Soon your personal relationships are as strained as your professional ones.

Plan your day. Know what a perfect day should look like, and what you want to accomplish in that day. Make your "to do" list, plan your meetings, and set your boundaries on your personal space. Then enjoy all that additional time doing your favorite things with your favorite people.

Chapter 18: Other Useful Tips for Maximizing Your To-Do List

The following three tips are actually lifestyle choices. What are lifestyle choices? Lifestyle choices are decisions that you make as an individual in regards to how you live your life and behave based upon your attitudes, tastes, and values according to the Oxford Dictionaries. As you're going through life, you've made choices on what you'll eat, where you'll eat, where you'll work, how long you'll work, whether you'll have children or not, etc. These are all lifestyle choices based upon your attitudes, tastes, and values. However, your choices may not all be productive choices. Why should you make productive lifestyle choices? Making healthy and productive lifestyle choices will enable to you feel your best and be your most productive resulting in the enhancement of our time management skills.

The best way to ensure that you use your time to your advantage is to develop a routine. If every day you get up and do the same things, you'll know how long it takes you to complete each activity, you won't forget something, and the rest of the individuals in your home will be less likely to vary from the routine and mess up your day.

For example, I'll take you through the first 30 minutes of my morning, I hit my snooze button one time before dragging my tired self-up, then go to the kitchen to crack open a Diet Pepsi as I can't function without the illusion that the caffeine is helping. After taking a long drink and eating a handful of M&M's, I head into the bathroom to turn on the heater so it'll warm up the room before my shower. After the heater gets going, I spend 10 minutes in meditation before reading some inspirational messages and then hit the shower. Knowing how long it takes to complete each activity is invaluable for the times that the youngest decides that she needs to wake up three times and the last time for a two-hour marathon from 2 o'clock to 4 o'clock. After an hour of trying to get her to sleep with her saying "I'm done. Can I watch your phone?", I gave up, handed her my phone, and chewed a gummy melatonin. The melatonin was a mistake. Or was it?

I did get up an hour late. However, I was able to realize how fast I could get myself and everyone else ready-40 minutes when it normally takes me 1 hour and 45 minutes. On top of that, I didn't forget anything and as the schedule of activities was exactly the same, only quicker, no one else interfered with the morning routine.

The second lifestyle choice is to be organized. Everything has its place. If you're diligent about having a place for everything and putting it where it belongs, then you can avoid countless hours in a week of looking for things. I have a family member who's always late. But, I've seen his house, so I don't question why he's late. There's no order for where he puts things each night. One day, his car keys might be in his bedroom under a dirty shirt and his wallet might be tossed on the kitchen counter amongst the canned goods that he purchased the previous weekend. The next day, his keys and wallet might be hidden under a newspaper by his television remotes. Not being able to find the things that you need to be able to leave the house every morning causes unnecessary stress and speeding tickets. Find a place where you're going to house your daily essentials and put them there as soon as you're done with them each day. You'll save so much time and have peace of mind.

Being organized at work can be a huge time saver as well. When your supervisor calls and asks for a document that came out the year prior and you know exactly which folder it's in-is golden. I had a previous employee that I'm not sure how she got anything done as her office looked like a tornado hit every day. At least it wasn't a sharknado, all of the blood and chunks would have probably took the mess to the point of no return. Granted, she had an idea where everything was, but had to sift through all of the piles each time she needed to find something and a stiff wind would have been put her into an unnecessary crisis. Get a bunch of file folders. Put labels on the tops and file items in their respective places when you receive them. It might take time at the beginning, but it'll save you tons later on.

That reminds me of a story of how being organized would have saved me a ton of time. My brother and I decided to stain our deck. Instead of spending the extra time putting plastic or cardboard between the deck and the siding of our new house, we decided just to spray away. Kind of lazy on our part, because we actually had the plastic and some boxes that I half *ss tried to use. However, they wouldn't stay put and would have required me to actually use tape and take my time. So, I tossed them to the side and grabbed the spray gun. An hour later, we had our rather large deck stained. Yippee!

On to the not so happy part, after waiting a day to let the floor dry, we discovered that we had an abundance of overspray on the siding and it was stuck on good. I tried to use mineral spirits, but each pencil tip dot required scrubbing. Elbow scrubbing. After putting "cleaning the siding" onto my "when I can get to it" list for a month, I decided I would try again. One excruciating hour later, I had managed to get one row of siding cleared off with about 20 left to go. At my brother's insistence, we headed to the internet to see if there was anything else that might work to get the stain off of the siding. Paint thinner. Unfortunately, we live in a small town and the only store that was open didn't care paint thinner. We eventually tried gasoline. Thank God. It took five more hours, but we had it cleaned off. The moral of the story is that if I would have been organized prior to staining the deck, I could have saved myself seven to eight hours, not to mention, all of the time I spent looking at the siding and heading back into the house to ignore the problem.

The last tip is to learn to say "no". Are you the one that signed up for all three of your kids' holiday parties (a different holiday for each one and for games no less), because the lines were still blank when it was your turn to mark the volunteer box off for the "back to school night" treasure hunt? Did you agree to take the kids around to all of the shops in town to try and sell fundraiser tickets, because the paper said that the shop workers really enjoy seeing the kids smiling faces? Are you the Vice President of your office Personnel Club making decisions no one will be happy with when making end of the year holiday plans? When your boss asked for volunteers to work extra hours on the new marketing project did your traitorous hand shoot up like it had a life of its own? Me, me, me.

Now, take a moment to determine why you feel the need to do this. Guilt? The need for recognition? Fear of letting someone down? Fear of speaking up? You think everyone else is doing it, so you feel obligated? Would you jump off a bridge if your friends did? Sorry, I heard my mom's voice in my head for a second there.

Once you've discovered the reason that you're never saying "no", identify the things that you should really be saying "no" to and put your foot down. Or, as the saying goes, grab ahold of your ears and pull your head out of your *ss. If you're struggling with figuring out what you should be saying "no" to, go back to your number one priority and ask "Is doing this getting me closer to or further away from my priority?" Saying "no" is not a crime. Maybe you truly want to do some of these things. Good. Go ahead and do them, but not all of them and not at the expense of your number one priority. You might even find that it is exhilarating to throw those pieces of paper into the trash when they come home in your child's backpack.

Key Take Always:

- **Develop a routine.** This will ensure that you use your time to the best of your ability.

- **Be organized.** Everything has its place. If you're diligent about having a place for everything and put it where it belongs, then you can avoid countless hours in a week looking for things.

- **Learn to say "no".** Identify the reason that you have the uncontrollable desire to say "yes" to everything. Once you've identified the reason, spend some time identifying which things are taking you away from your priority and put your foot down.

Conclusion

Thank you for making it through to the end of To Do List Formula guide.

The next step is to practice what you have learned in this book and apply these tips and concepts out in the real world. Time management is a necessary tool for success in whatever goals you want to achieve in life; it correlated to success. You are now fully aware of the bad habits that hinder successful time management, such as procrastination, not setting the right goal, as well as multitasking, so you can now avoid these habits to occur—that is if you really focus on the goal and not be complacent. Also be mindful of properly setting up your daily life schedule, which is a very important step for you to have a guide. Time management and planning requires us to record events in which, aside from using the old method of pen and paper, we can now record and create a schedule using apps and software on various devices because of today's technological advancement.

Remember that time management is a continuous process, as well as planning and scheduling. These things will help measure your routine in life in order to boost your productivity in your workplace, at home, and even in your personal life. I hope you learned a lot from my experiences.

Printed in Great Britain
by Amazon

18069613R00078